Cambridge

MW00345833

Elements in Business Strategy
edited by
J.-C. Spender
Rutgers Business School

WHAT EVERY CEO SHOULD KNOW ABOUT AI

Viktor Dörfler
University of Strathclyde Business School

CAMBRIDGE
UNIVERSITY PRESS

CAMBRIDGE
UNIVERSITY PRESS

University Printing House, Cambridge CB2 8BS, United Kingdom

One Liberty Plaza, 20th Floor, New York, NY 10006, USA

477 Williamstown Road, Port Melbourne, VIC 3207, Australia

314–321, 3rd Floor, Plot 3, Splendor Forum, Jasola District Centre, New Delhi – 110025, India

103 Penang Road, #05–06/07, Visioncrest Commercial, Singapore 238467

Cambridge University Press is part of the University of Cambridge.

It furthers the University's mission by disseminating knowledge in the pursuit of education, learning, and research at the highest international levels of excellence.

www.cambridge.org
Information on this title: www.cambridge.org/9781009016926
DOI: 10.1017/9781009037853

First published 2022

A catalogue record for this publication is available from the British Library.

ISBN 978-1-009-01692-6 Paperback
ISSN 2515-0693 (online)
ISSN 2515-0685 (print)

What Every CEO Should Know About AI

Elements in Business Strategy

DOI: 10.1017/9781009037853
First published online: February 2022

Viktor Dörfler
University of Strathclyde Business School
Author for correspondence: Viktor Dörfler, ai@ViktorDorfler.com

Abstract: Dr. Viktor Dörfler combines his background in developing and implementing AI with scholarly research on knowledge and cultivating talent to address misconceptions about AI. The Element explains what AI can and cannot do, carefully delineating facts from beliefs or wishful thinking. Filled with examples, this practical Element is thought-provoking. The purpose is to help CEOs figure out how to make the best use of AI, suggesting how to extract AI's greatest value through appropriate task allocation between human experts and AI. The author challenges the attribution of characteristics like understanding, thinking, and creativity to AI, supporting his argument with the ideas of the finest AI philosophers. He also discusses in depth one of the most sensitive AI-related topics: ethics. The readers are encouraged to make up their own minds about AI and draw their own conclusions rather than accepting opinions from people with vested interests or an agenda.

Keywords: artificial intelligence, expert systems, knowledge-based strategizing, intuition, personal knowledge

ISBNs: 9781009016926 (PB), 9781009037853 (OC)
ISSNs: 2515-0693 (online), 2515-0685 (print)

Contents

Foreword

This book is rare in several ways and unique in its combination of attributes. First, few, if any, books are aimed specifically at the CEO or senior executive who wants to learn about artificial intelligence. Fewer still are so admirably concise.

The content is unique in that it combines AI, knowledge and knowledge work, and business strategy. There are books that relate AI to strategy – I wrote one of them – but none that relate it to knowledge and knowledge work. If there were any, I would be aware of them, because I did a lot of work in knowledge management ten to twenty years ago, and I keep an eye out for anything that brings that topic into present times. This is somewhat curious, as AI is about embedding knowledge into computer systems, and often the target is the human knowledge worker, both for extracting their knowledge and for automating their key tasks.

Finally, the book is unique in that it looks simultaneously into the history and the future of AI. Unlike most books on AI, the author, Professor Dörfler, has worked in the AI field for many years and is familiar with the many winters and springs the field has endured. It is truly unusual, for example, to find an author who can compare expert systems to deep learning neural networks.

Why, you ask, should a busy senior executive be interested in learning about AI's past? Only because AI's past is likely to be its future – once again. Neural networks were given up for dead in the 1960s, then arose in the late 1980s and early 1990s for fraud identification in financial services. By the turn of the century, the world had largely lost interest in them again, though financial services firms still made very effective use of them. They arose again in the 2010s in the form of deep learning neural networks. Now these are perhaps the single most popular technique in all of AI. There were small advances that enabled their rebirth each time, but the basic principles remained the same.

The same historical rebirth could also happen with rule-based expert systems, a technology with which the author is quite familiar because he created a tool for developing them. Expert systems were the AI technology in the late 1980s and early 1990s. Like neural networks, they beat on in the hearts of insurance underwriting systems, healthcare clinical decision support, and multiple other applications. Yet to the press and many AI experts, they were declared dead long ago.

Dörfler is well aware of the strengths and weaknesses of logic-based expert systems, and he makes a good case that they will reappear in the future of AI. Some of the greatest AI researchers in the world have acknowledged that deep learning models are not enough to power the many future uses of AI, and the simplicity, causality, and explainability of rule-based systems are likely to bring about their return.

Don't read this book if you are only looking for what is most fashionable about AI. But if you desire to know the essence of AI – how it can capture, analyze, and apply knowledge to problems that humans need to solve – you have picked up the correct little tome. You will gain much wisdom about knowledge and intelligence – human and artificial – if you keep it in your hands or on your screen and turn its pages until the end.

Thomas H. Davenport
Distinguished Professor, Babson College and Visiting Professor,
Oxford Saïd Business School
Fellow, MIT Initiative on the Digital Economy
and Senior Advisor to Deloitte AI
Author of *Competing on Analytics* and *The AI Advantage*

1 Introduction: The Strategic Landscape of AI

Prediction is very difficult, especially if it's about the future!

Niels Bohr[1]

There is little doubt today about the significance of artificial intelligence (AI), but it is less clear why it should have a place in a series on business strategy. The book's title suggests that there is something that every CEO should know about AI – does this mean even those who do not intend to use AI? Definitely yes. And in this short book I explain why.

To avoid any confusion, it is important to clarify my position from the outset. I am an AI enthusiast, and I believe that AI can be an incredibly useful thing if we figure out how to use it well. However, I am not a carnival barker[2] who just wants everyone's buy-in, regardless of whether AI is useful for the particular topic or not. Conversely, I am also not a harbinger of doom foretelling how AI will overtake the world and enslave or exterminate humankind. This book depicts the limitations as well as the strengths of AI and delineates facts from beliefs in order to make it possible for CEOs to decide in particular situations whether they need AI and how to use it.

1.1 AI, Strategy, and the CEO

How do we know that AI is important? As with not only any technology but any phenomenon in the world, we can look for the money. AI seems to be the most expensive human endeavor ever; the four most prominent hubs – the US, the UK, Canada, and Israel – together spent well over a trillion dollars on AI, and China, India, and Russia are probably not far behind. Chengwei Liu suggested in *AoM Insight* (2020) that the first trillionaire in the world would come about from the AI business. We can also see that AI is ubiquitous; it permeates all areas of our work as well as our private lives. This takes us to the very reason why every CEO needs to know something about AI: It is not possible to opt out. In 1997, on the Oracle Co. website, a statement appeared: "In five years nobody will call it e-business. It will simply be business." It took a little longer, but it happened. Similarly, AI is not optional; if a company does not adopt it, its competitors will, customers may expect it, etc., so not using AI does not mean one is not affected by it.

---

[1] This saying is perhaps most often attributed to the Nobel Prize–winning physicist, but variants also appear with attributions to Samuel Goldwyn, K. K. Steincke, Robert Storm Petersen, Yogi Berra, Mark Twain, and even Nostradamus. It is also quoted as "an old Danish proverb," but it seems to be a proverb that cannot be traced.

[2] "a . . . person who attempts to attract patrons to entertainment events, such as a circus or funfair" (Wikipedia: barker).

In contrast to what we may learn from (technology) management textbooks or academic journal papers, in real-world organizations CEOs seem to be invested in ICT (information communication technology) decisions. So why is a CIO, even if there is one, not in charge of an ERP (enterprise resource planning) decision? The reason is that such decisions are never mere technical decisions. The CEO of British Petroleum said a couple of decades ago that in ICT investments, about 20 percent of the cost is the hardware and the software and 80 percent is learning and cultural change. That is, such decisions affect businesses at their very core; it changes how they see themselves and their environments. In other words, it affects their Theory of the Firm (ToF). Thus what each CEO should know about AI is how it affects their ToF and the actions stemming from their ToF – their business strategy.

The purpose of this book is to deliver exactly that. While CEOs do not need to understand the technical details of AI, they can benefit from understanding what sorts of AI there are and what each sort can be expected to deliver. In other words, it is useful if a CEO is able to see through the too often overly enthusiastic dreams of AI researchers, as well as the excessive claims of AI vendors, in order to make informed strategic decisions – as well as to decide in broad terms how to go about the implementation. The final decisions can most meaningfully be taken at the deep levels of the corporate hierarchy, where the relevant knowledge resides. This is in line with Charles Handy's (2015) principle of inverse delegation, meaning that the decisions belong where the knowledge is, and if help is needed, the specialists delegate to their bosses.

This book is not only aimed at CEOs; anyone working with and for a CEO can benefit from it. This means that AI researchers and AI vendors will also benefit from it, as they will learn about the context and potential values as well as the pitfalls of AI. AI vendors cannot decide for a client where and for what purpose it needs AI, as they do not understand the primary business processes of their clients in depth. Clients also have problems with these decisions, as they do not know what AI can deliver. This is the age-old problem of ICT implementation; what is sold is different from what is purchased. The vendor sells the capabilities of the product, while clients purchase solutions to their problems. For a successful implementation, these two need to be brought together, which will require a collaboration between a subject expert from the client and an AI expert from the vendor. In order to develop a conceptual and cultural framework in which this is possible, it is useful if the CEO is able to distinguish between facts and beliefs in AI, thus understanding the value AI can realistically deliver.

As indicated above, besides CEOs, this book is primarily relevant to those who work with CEOs. However, in a sense, all of us work with CEOs, and most of this book is about understanding how AI affects our lives, in a strategic sense, and how to make the best use of it. In this sense, this book is a brief summary of what we need to think through when we have the chance to use an AI solution and how to use it for the greatest benefit – whatever that may be. Therefore, this book is not about giving the readers the answers but about showing how they can obtain their own answers. Unfortunately – or perhaps fortunately – generic, universally applicable solutions do not exist. As in most cases with reference to strategy, everyone must find their own.

1.2 Uncertainty: The Context of Strategy

To set the scene for thinking strategically about AI, we need to depict the landscape in which businesses exist as *uncertainty*, as reconceptualized by Frank Knight (1921) and as extended and enriched by J. C. Spender over the past fifty years (Spender, 2021). Uncertainty is characterized by knowledge absences (Spender, 2014), and these knowledge absences create opportunity spaces (Spender, 2021). The essence of entrepreneurial and managerial work is to construct a language that makes engaging with the opportunity spaces possible, rendering them actionable and manageable. In this context, AI is useful if it helps us wrestle with these knowledge absences.

Knight introduced the concept of uncertainty to contrast it with the concept of risk. In the case of risk, although we do not know exactly what will happen as a consequence of a decision, we have complete knowledge of all the alternatives that may happen as well as of the probabilities of each of the alternatives, which together add up to 100 percent; in other words, the probability distribution is known. In uncertainty, we do not have such complete knowledge; we have knowledge absences. These knowledge absences can be of different kinds.

Martin Shubik (1954) distinguished two aspects of uncertainty: *ignorance* and *indeterminacy*. Ignorance stands for what could in principle be known, only the CEO does not know. It could be information that exists but is not accessible to the CEO, or it could be infeasible or even impossible to obtain, as there is a great deal of information. In contrast, indeterminacy brings in the other players. Indeterminacy is not about knowledge that is difficult to access or obtain; the knowledge, in this case, does not exist. Typical examples are the competitors, who pursue their respective courses of action and whose behavior is not fully determined by the rules of the game – which leads to the area of game theory,[3] which is Shubik's primary

---

[3] Game theory is a discipline of applied mathematics, pioneered by John von Neumann (von Neumann & Morgenstern, 1953), that depicts strategic situations in economics, politics, etc. as games, i.e. using mathematical models that involve multiple (rational) decision makers, referred to as players, that make choices independently of each other but in response to each other, and the outcomes of their choices are affected by the other players' choices.

field.[4] Indeterminacy might more colloquially be thought of as *free will*. Spender (2014) further extended the model by adding *incommensurability*, meaning that the players, as well as knowledge items, cannot be compared, as they are so different that we even lack the basis for comparison. Incommensurability could also be termed *uniqueness*. More recently, Spender (2018) identified another aspect of uncertainty, which he calls *irrelevance*. The core argument here is that the information that we can express in a (formal) language may be less relevant to the phenomenon at hand and our decision regarding it than what we cannot verbalize. This means that the tacit dimension of personal knowledge (Polányi, 1962a, 1966b) is more relevant than explicit knowledge, which is why this aspect of uncertainty might also be called *tacit knowledge*.

In order to improve the orientation around the concepts of uncertainty, my coauthor Alina Bas and I (Dörfler & Bas, unpublished) organized these concepts into three realms: *known, unknown*, and *unknowable*.[5] *Known* refers to complete knowledge, therefore it includes risk as well as the special case of risk – certainty, where there is only one alternative with 100 percent probability. Importantly, risk is not less known than certainty; in both cases there is complete knowledge, but in "certainty" it is a complete knowledge of a specific outcome, while in the case of "risk" it is a complete knowledge of the probability distribution. Unknown and unknowable together comprise uncertainty, which is bound by the knowns. Spender notes that the knowns are also not as well-behaved as some may wish, as they can be "surprising, ambiguous, anomalous, inconsistent, or contradictory" (Spender, 2021: 129). *Unknown* corresponds to ignorance; that which is possible to know, but which the CEO just does not know here and now. *Unknowable*, in contrast, means that it is impossible to know; it covers uniqueness, free will, and tacit knowledge (or in Spender's terminology incommensurability, indeterminacy, and irrelevance).

Importantly, uncertainty does not mean that the CEO does not know any-thing. As Shubik wrote: "It is fairly obvious that there is rarely an economic situation in which the entrepreneur has no information at all. If such a situation

---

[4] Spender warns that "game theory only offers rigorous solutions when there is no uncertainty left, when each player's moves can be 'gamed out'" (Spender, 2021: 128). For us this is important, as we cannot simply leave this up to AI, as this can perhaps work well in a simulation, but in the context of the CEO's reality, there is always some uncertainty left, so a rigorous solution is impossible.

[5] This is not the same as Donald Rumsfeld's "known unknowns" and "unknown unknowns"; those are both unknowns. Sometimes we may know of what it is what we do not know, at other times we may not, but in both cases it is not a matter of learning it; the knowledge is unobtainable.

exists, then the first action of the entrepreneur must be to obtain information" (Shubik, 1954: 632).

For instance, the CEO may know about alternatives A-B-C, and may know that A is more likely than B and B is more likely than C, without being able to allocate exact percentages, and there may be further alternatives beyond the CEO's grasp and some of these may be more likely than A. In most cases it is also reasonably safe to assume that the tax regulation, for instance, will not change; that is, it is known. Perhaps even more importantly, more than one of the four aspects of uncertainty can, and usually do, affect the CEO at the same time: There is often inaccessible information or information that cannot be processed sufficiently quickly (ignorance), there are often several or even many players (uniqueness) making their own decisions (free will), and the CEO has a feel regarding where the industry is going, the mood of the competitors, etc. (tacit knowledge).

Elsewhere we suggested that AI can be a good tool for the unknown, but to cope with the unknowable, CEOs use their intuition (Dörfler & Bas, 2020b). We can refine this argument. AI can be exceptionally useful in the realm of the unknown, but it cannot do the job on its own. As Spender eloquently put it: "Firms are contexts in which data-driven theorizing is subordinated to entrepreneurial judgment. . . . As we collide with the uncertainties that arrest our activity, we respond with imagination rather than with reason" (Spender, 2021: 125).

At the end of the day, the CEO will still need to make decisions, but AI can provide useful information for those decisions if we figure out how to use it in a sensible way. In the realm of the unknowable, CEOs will have to rely on their intuition, but AI may be useful, for example, in helping to identify the scope for intuiting, as long as it is a unique AI setup for the specific organization at hand and subordinated to the CEO's value judgment. I return to these points in Section 7.

1.3 Why This Book?

In 2017 the MIT Sloan Management Review and the Boston Consulting Group together surveyed 3,000 executives, managers, and analysts across a variety of industries and conducted in-depth interviews with 30+ technology experts and executives (Ransbotham et al., 2017). They found the following:

> The gap between ambition and execution is large at most companies. Three-quarters of executives believe AI will enable their companies to move into new businesses. Almost 85% believe AI will allow their companies to obtain or sustain a competitive advantage. But only about one in five companies has

incorporated AI in some offerings or processes. Only one in 20 companies
has extensively incorporated AI in offerings or processes. Less than 39% of
all companies have an AI strategy in place. The largest companies – those
with at least 100,000 employees – are the most likely to have an AI strategy,
but only half have one. (Ransbotham et al., 2017: 1)

This issue is addressed within this book, which is somewhat but not quite entirely
unique. This book is about the most advanced technology, yet it is nontechnologi-
cal. It is primarily written for top executives (and my MBA class) so that they can
learn about technology, but it will be equally useful for technical people, as they will
understand the business strategy mindset a little bit better within the context of AI.
There are numerous books and papers that explore the use of AI by business
organizations, but they usually focus on what is available, and often within the
context of one narrow functional area, such as finance or marketing. In contrast, this
book approaches the organization as a whole and focuses on the strategic thinking
process of making use of AI. The book that comes closest to this approach is
Thomas Davenport's (2018) *The AI Advantage*; however, that book focuses more
on the analytical aspect, and therefore the two can be regarded as complementary.

This book depicts a particular picture of AI at a relatively high level of abstraction, often exaggerating or simplifying issues in order to make them easier to
understand – but carefully, so as to be correct in principle. As such, it offers more
of a "big picture painted with a thick brush and broad brushstrokes"; that is, it is
a comprehensive picture that lacks many details but from which the picture can be
recognized. For this reason, although the book talks about artificial intelligence
throughout, there is perhaps more psychology and philosophy than technology
included. As often happens with relatively new and incompletely understood
ideas still in development, in order to understand what they are, it is useful to
delineate them from and even contrast them to what they are not. As the area is
complex and changing fast, many details are perhaps omitted from the text and not
all details are up to date; however, the details that become available will easily find
their ways to anyone's attention, so this is not as important. The most important role
of such "big-picture" books is to help the reader develop their own thinking about
these issues in the way that suits them. Many arguments are offered, but more
important are the ways in which they are constructed; showing this helps the reader
construct their own argument. Having the big picture as a reference point, readers
will find it easy to make sense not only of what is already there about AI but also
what will come about in the future.

Having written this book for CEOs does not only refer to the content but also
to its style. The text is organized into five substantive sections, each consisting
of five subsections. Four subsections in each section are around 1,000 words,
and each can mostly be read on its own. This does not mean that there is no

progression in the book or that the subsections do not connect – they do, but they can be read individually or a couple of them at a time and then be continued later. The fifth subsection in each section is called "So What?"; these are sort of takeaway points; something you can take with you if you plan to discuss AI or to serve as a brief recap. The reason for designing the text this way was to try to adapt to the busy schedules of my readers.

The first section, "Ex Machina," is the most technical one; this introduces the different types of AI. It is important for CEOs to have a nuanced and complete picture regarding what is out there. The next three sections deal with the most important human aspects of what we associate with intelligence; knowing, learning, and creating. Each compares and contrasts human ways with machine ways. The most significant takeaways from each section are the aspects on deciding what to use AI for and where we need human experts. The last section focuses on the ethical aspects of AI. This is the most dynamic area of AI at this time; we come across new moral dilemmas associated with AI on a daily basis. Therefore, by the time the reader gets into this book, there will be novel moral issues not covered – but the hope is to provide a solid basis for tackling these mindfully. I also believe it is in the area of ethics, rather than technology, where we will learn the most about AI over the next decade or so. In Section 7, I will get back to the issues that I brought up in Section 1: namely, how AI can help CEOs cope with uncertainty.

2 Ex Machina

Any sufficiently advanced technology is indistinguishable from magic.

Arthur C. Clarke[6]

This section focuses on the different types of AI; each is explained in its respective historical context. The reason for including this historical perspective is that it helps us to understand what the particular AI types were supposed to accomplish, how they were expected to work, and what was their expected scope of validity. In other words, we should understand the assumptions behind the particular AI types and see what has changed since their inception. This section also helps us to develop a working AI vocabulary, demystifying concepts like "deep learning" and explaining the technological background in fairly understandable, nontechnical terms. Although this is not necessary for CEOs in order to think about AI, it is very useful when it comes to communicating about AI, particularly if it is with people who are "high tech native," who were born familiar with today's information technology. An important complementary read to this section is Pamela McCorduck's (2004) personal review of AI history, which is rooted in interviews with many of the early AI gurus. I see things somewhat differently and make my case below, but the richness of McCorduck's story is admirable. This section also retells some history, elaborating on the origins of the different types of AI and helping to uncover the underlying assumptions about them.

2.1 Symbolic Reasoning Systems

According to AI folklore, the history of AI started in January 1956 when Herbert Simon taught his first class on Mathematical Models in the Social Sciences at the Carnegie Institute of Technology (today Carnegie-Mellon University), having just returned from the New Year holiday. It was a working holiday, as he told his students: "Over the Christmas holiday, Al Newell and I invented a thinking machine" (Simon, 1991: 206). One of the students in the class was Edward Feigenbaum, who recounts that this sentence made him so excited about the topic that he became Simon's PhD student (Feigenbaum, 1992: 3). Later we saw Feigenbaum become the father of another type of AI, but for now, we stick with Newell and Simon.

The "thinking machine" that Newell and Simon created, together with Cliff Shaw from the RAND Corporation, was called the Logic Theorist, or Logic Theory Machine (Newell & Simon, 1956). Just to hint about the state of technology at the time, Newell and Simon had to fly to Los Angeles to do this

---

[6] This statement became popular as Clarke's Third Law (originally published in Clarke, 1962).

work, as that was where the RAND Corporation gave them access to a computer – a power-hungry IBM 701[7] with less than 20 kB memory (your laptop has about a million times more), using unreliable vacuum tubes and costing millions of dollars – universities did not have computers; they could not afford them.

The purpose of the Logic Theorist was ambitious: "it was devised to learn how it is possible to solve difficult problems such as proving mathematical theorems, discovering scientific laws from data, playing chess, or understanding the meaning of English prose" (Newell et al., 1963: 109). Continuing this line of thought, the Logic Theory Machine project evolved into the more ambitious General Problem Solver (GPS), which was supposed to extend this scope to any and all areas of human problem-solving. This type of AI was also the first attempt at what is today referred to as "wide AI" or, at its extreme, Artificial General Intelligence (AGI).

The idea behind the Logic Theory Machine and the GPS was sound – as an idea. Simon and Newell's initial intention was to understand or "model" the human mind. They used a computer simulation. Listening to the presentation of Oliver Selfridge (1955) on symbol manipulation and pattern recognition in computers (Newell said this could have been called AI already: see McCorduck, 2004), a more ambitious plan started to take shape in Allen Newell's mind. If all human problem-solving could be represented as symbol manipulation, and if computers could manipulate symbols and identify patterns, then machines should be able to solve real-world problems, not only arithmetic problems. This would be achieved by following the steps of human problem-solving in order to replicate the outcomes (i.e. solutions to the problems). The essence of the idea was that by collecting the steps of problem-solving in many areas, it should be possible to extract the general principles of reasoning, and by applying these principles and generic steps, AI would not only work within a narrow, well-defined scope but across many domains. In order to capture the steps of human problem-solving, experts were asked to use a "thinking aloud" technique; that is, to say and record what they thought. Remarkably, they were expected to include even the mistakes they made, as those might be useful or even necessary parts of the overall problem-solving process.

The idea was brilliant and was a radical departure from the computerized problem-solving approaches of the time. The "normal" approach would have been to consider a problem in its entirety at a sufficient level of detail, which allowed for some sort of optimization or operational research (OR) method. In contrast, the new approach held the promise of being able to engage in

---

[7] Newell, Simon, and Shaw used the computer nicknamed "Johnniac" after John von Neumann.

a problem-solving process when it was not even clear whether there was a solution or how many solutions there could be. The performance delivered by the Logic Theorist was amazing; eventually, it proved 38 of the first 52 theorems in the *Principia Mathematica*[8] (Simon, 1995), and Simon found the proof to theorem 2.85 to be more elegant than the one produced by Whitehead and Russell. Russell was delighted to hear this (McCorduck, 2004: 167, footnote).

The achievements of the Logic Theorist are fascinating, and its creators even more so. However, some of the assumptions and implications are problematic. The underlying assumption was that there are general principles of problem-solving; some line of reasoning that would only differ in its detail. Considering the breadth of the scope of human problem-solving, can we really expect that there are some generic steps that apply from kissing to cooking a stew, and also to designing a car or composing music? I do not believe that there are, and if there were, they would be so hopelessly generic that we could not really apply them. As a matter of fact, when using machine learning to figure out the rules of a particular person's book preferences, it became clear that different rules apply to the categories of "fantasy" and "sci-fi," not to mention the radically different rules of what makes a good crime novel in the mind of the same person. Nothing indicates that there is a generic way of problem-solving, even for one person, let alone for all of us. Next, while it may sound plausible that reasoning can be represented through the manipulation of symbols, this is not a fact. There is a sequence of logical steps in each (or at least most) line of reasoning that can be handled this way, but prior to applying those steps, we make assumptions – these are often not made explicit, and thus it may not be possible to describe them in the same way as the steps of reasoning. However, if all these assumptions hold (if not justified, they can still be correct), there is nothing to suggest that playing chess or proving theorems, which may arguably involve explicit logical steps, have anything in common with, for example, "understanding the meaning of English prose" or anything that involves the achievement of meaning. To be fair, we do not even know what it means to "understand the meaning" (cf. Winograd, 1980) – how could we teach a computer to do this? This point will be revisited in the next section (subsection 3.4) when discussing the AI knowledge problem.

The Logic Theorist was an amazing achievement of human creativity. It delivered an impressive performance, not to mention that it became the

---

[8] Foundational work in modern symbolic logic by Alfred North Whitehead and Bertrand Russell (1927).

history-making first instance of operational AI. This now-celebrated achievement was not so clearly praised from the outset, however. The same year that Simon reported the invention of the "thinking machine," a two-month workshop was organized at Dartmouth College. This workshop was a milestone in the history of AI in its own right, where McCarthy coined the term "Artificial Intelligence." Newell and Simon presented the Logic Theorist. The response to their "thinking machine" was underwhelming. Simon said he and Newell had already done what the others in the conference were only talking about, yet they did not seem impressed.

2.2 Symbolic Expert Systems

Having completed his PhD (more about this in subsection 3.4), Feigenbaum moved to Berkeley, away from the direct influence of Simon and Newell. He got back to his old obsession with machine performance, hoping to build a super-intelligent machine with a performance equal or even superior to that of human experts. Therefore, he abandoned the general principles of reasoning and the information-processing models and started to focus on heuristics and narrow domains of expertise. He figured that as it is experts who deliver high perform-ance in their respective domains, specialist knowledge must play an important role. He concluded that the computer must have a representation of the problem; some internal "model" of the external environment that was being reasoned. He speculated that such knowledge representations should be inductive. The pre-vailing AI methods were good at deductive reasoning but not at inductive, so he decided to focus on induction. Then he figured he should work with scientists whom he regarded as "professional inducers." This description may seem like a sequence of logical steps, but it looks like it was more of an intuitive leap: "These were overly simplistic intuitions and speculations. They could have been wildly wrong. But they were right. The 'work with scientists' intuition was one of the most fruitful I have ever had" (Feigenbaum, 1992: 7).

As he began working with scientists, focusing on induction, Feigenbaum anchored his project in experimental design; then any machine he and his team produced could be adequately tested. He decided on the problem of hypothesis formation and sought a partner and a task in the natural science world. At a gathering of people interested in AI at Stanford, he met Nobel Laureate Joshua Lederberg, the chair of Stanford's Genetics Department. They started discuss-ing what they could do together, and a few months later, Feigenbaum moved to Stanford. Lederberg suggested a topic from exobiology (the study of extrater-restrial life) rather than one from his own field of genetics, specifically about inducing molecular topologies from mass spectra. The project was supporting the Mars probe into life, or the precursors of life, on Mars. The input data was reliable, the calculations needed were beyond the usual but not beyond the AI capabilities of the time, and there was a chance to test the findings empirically.

The DENDRAL project performed two steps. First, it generated a large number of "topologically legal" candidate structures (based on valence), and then these were filtered to "chemically plausible" ones based on mass spectra. The second step required significant expertise in interpreting mass spectra. The project ran for many years, involving more and more experts, eventually covering a larger area than the knowledge of any of the individual experts. Finally, the program was performing on a par with and exceeding the work of top experts.

The reason that I went into such detail describing the process that led to the birth of DENDRAL is not my love for the historical process – although I do like the story. The reason is that I can now point out that little has changed since the time of the first knowledge-based expert system. Feigenbaum was meticulous in selecting a suitable problem for which to build this type of AI; the problem was of the right size and the right level of complexity, experts were available, and there was a possibility of checking the outcome (cf. Velencei, 2017). Having spent a great deal of time over the past 25 years supporting executives with a knowledge-based expert system, I can confirm that this is exactly how we still do it. Experts are essential; there is no expert system without experts. If we take a problem that is too complex, the experts will not be able to articulate their knowledge for us to model. This happened to us when we looked into the possibility of building an expert system for the maintenance of a nuclear power plant. If the problem is too simple, there is not much to put into the knowledge base, not to mention that there may not be experts at all. Plus Lederberg was a great partner of choice; he suggested a topic that was a perfect fit for the purpose, based on his project but not from his discipline (genetics). In fact, many years later he suggested that genetics was at the point where it could make sense to build an expert system for it (Feigenbaum, 2006: 20:50–21:45).

The DENDRAL project became the first knowledge-based expert system. A system being "knowledge-based" refers to the internal model called "knowledge representation," which was stored in the form of a "knowledge base," while the term "expert system" signifies that expert knowledge was being modeled. In its initial form, the knowledge representation in DENDRAL was stored in the form of lists in a specialized language called LISP. However, as more and more knowledge was added, the complexity increased and started to threaten the stability of the system. In the meantime, Newell and Simon made further progress in modeling memory and developed the model of memory called "productions." Adopting this approach, Bruce Buchanan, Feigenbaum's long-term collaborator, reprogrammed the system, establishing what became the standard for knowledge bases; the "production rules" or "if . . . then" rules, organized in a hierarchy.

The knowledge representation in an expert system is obtained in the process of *knowledge acquisition*, which is a subset of the overall process of *knowledge engineering*. To emphasize the central role, as well as to depict the nature of knowledge engineering, Feigenbaum (1977) called it "the art of AI." From the outset, Feigenbaum believed that knowledge representation was the most important part of the expert system. He expressed this in the "knowledge is power hypothesis"; later he claimed that there was so much evidence in support of this hypothesis that he changed it to the Knowledge Principle (Lenat & Feigenbaum, 1991).

In contrast to the reasoning systems, there do not appear to have been any assumptions that were not justified in the setup of expert systems. Furthermore, Feigenbaum seems to have got everything right the first time, for little has changed since that time. When speculating about the future of expert systems, Feigenbaum (1992: 16) described two shortcomings: *brittleness* and *isolation*. The first one means that although expert systems deliver high performance in their narrow domains, they are completely useless even a tiny step beyond their domain's boundary, for there is then no nonspecialist knowledge to fall back on. The second means that expert systems were never brought together to collaborate and thus solve different and bigger problems. Based on these two shortcomings, he speculated that the second era of expert systems would involve large knowledge bases, knowledge sharing, and the interoperability of geographically distributed knowledge bases. With the Internet, the geographical distribution problem has disappeared. Interoperability is no longer an issue either; we can connect knowledge bases and even use one knowledge base as input for another. However, we still need to take note of the problem of large knowledge bases and knowledge sharing (these will be revisited in subsection 4.4).

Both symbolic systems – the reasoning and the expert systems – rely on symbol manipulation and need a form of knowledge acquisition to obtain the steps of reasoning or the knowledge representation respectively. There is a great divide between the two types of symbolic AI. While the purpose of reasoning systems was to create a domain-independent "generally intelligent" system (an AGI), the purpose of expert systems is to produce exceptional performance in well-defined narrow areas by modeling the subject-specific knowledge of experts.

Knowledge-based expert systems dominated the AI landscape until the mid-1980s, producing a large number of successful implementations in a wide range of areas from science and manufacturing through to medical treatments. At the same time, the symbolic reasoning approach did not produce any implementations that would work successfully across multiple domains, though some implementations were successful in narrow domains.

2.3 Artificial Neural Networks

While the symbolic approaches to AI (first the reasoning systems, later the expert systems) dominated the early days of AI, the connectionist approach, in its first incarnation, had been developed earlier. Warren McCulloch and Walter Pitts (1943) came up with a model of artificial neurons, synthesizing insights from the physiology and functioning of neurons, from Whitehead and Russell's (1927) propositional logic and from Turing's (1937) computation theory (see more details in Russell & Norvig, 2020). McCulloch and Pitts showed that any function could be calculated by an appropriate network of artificial neurons and further stipulated that, if suitably constructed, such networks could "learn." The first Artificial Neural Network (ANN) implementation, the SNARC (Stochastic Neural Analog Reinforcement Calculator), was done by Marvin Minsky and Dean Edmonds as part of their undergraduate work at Princeton in 1950. The purpose of the early ANNs was to demonstrate that any mathematical function could be calculated by a suitable network of artificial neurons; therefore, instead of regarding them as AI, they might be better described as "pre-AI."

Artificial Neural Networks became somewhat dormant until the mid-1980s, when they had a big comeback. There were several reasons for the timing of this comeback. First, the initial ANNs were just too power-hungry to be useful with the technology of the time. The SNARC consisted of 40 simulated neurons and used "3,000 vacuum tubes and a surplus automatic pilot mechanism from a B-24 bomber" (Russell & Norvig, 2020). By the mid-1980s, computers had become sufficiently fast to cope with ANNs of a useful size. Furthermore, by the mid-1980s, the symbolic approach was not delivering on the expectations. Expert systems were successful, but only in narrow domains. They took a long time (often an extremely long time) to develop, and many of them were already obsolete by the time the problem was solved, the decision made, or whatever the purpose of the particular expert system was. Today, expert systems are mainly used in supporting strategic decisions, where the price tag allows for the excessive cost, or for routine decisions that reliably do not change through a very large number of repetitions. The symbolic reasoning systems, though aiming to operate across domains, pursued the idea of AGI (artificial general intelligence) but only delivered results in narrow domains, for example, playing chess. Today, ANNs are the most-mentioned form of AI; they occupy much of the AI landscape, including the concept of machine learning (ML).

Therefore, what follows is a very simplified description of what ANNs are and how they work (based on Dörfler, 2020).

Any ANN consists of three sets of artificial neurons. There is an input layer that receives a signal (stimulus) – a stimulus can be more or less anything delivered in an electronic format. Then there is a hidden layer, which performs a translation or "black box" operation between the input and the output. Finally, the output layer produces a response to the stimulus received by the input layer. Nowadays we often hear terms like "deep ANN" or "deep learning," which sound mystical and exciting; in fact, these simply mean that there is more than one layer of artificial neurons in the hidden layer (LeCun et al., 2015). Computationally, the number of layers may make a difference, but logically the concepts are simple. The artificial neurons are connected to each other across the layers, like synapses in the human (or other) brain, hence the term "connectionist approach." Each connection has an initial weight, so as the stimulus "ignites" the system, the signal propagates towards the output neurons, resulting in a response. The response is compared to what was expected, the weights are adjusted, and the process is repeated iteratively. As it is easy to process a large number of learning samples (both stimuli and the desired responses), the ANN can relatively quickly adjust to producing the desired response. In other words, ANNs learn from the large number of learning examples how to reproduce their statistical frequency.

As the artificial neurons were modeled after the biological neurons, the ANN supposedly resembles the human brain. Therefore, so the argument goes, a sufficiently large ANN should be able to think. Furthermore, as the digital neurons are faster than the biological ones, by the same logic, these machines should be smarter than humans are. Let me unpack this argument's facts from its beliefs (see Ullman, 2019 for a more enthusiastic case but one that is very clear in delineating facts, beliefs, and hopes).

When it comes to an ANN, size does matter. The human brain is taken to consist of about 80–100 billion neurons, with around 7,000 connections on average, resulting in some 700–1,000 trillion (10^{15}) synapses in total. The largest ANNs today consist of about 16 million artificial neurons, which roughly corresponds to the size of a frog's brain. In terms of the number of synapses, we may be about 8–10 orders of magnitude short of the human brain's network. The other catch is that an ANN of 16 million artificial neurons would take a long time to train, even by the fastest supercomputers today. In addition, such an ANN would be so complicated that the architect could not grasp it anymore – the only way to analyze such a huge ANN would be by using AI. As such, it is unlikely that it is only a matter of time until we produce ANN of a similar size to the human brain, even despite the increase of 6 orders of magnitude over the past 70 years.

The structure of ANNs is also worth looking at. In ANNs, the connections usually only go forward, meaning that any artificial neuron only connects to the ones from the next layer (in some networks there can be within-layer connections as well). It is not clear that there are any circular connections in human brains, though we may know shortly. Furthermore, it is possible that we should not even think in terms of "layers" when it comes to the brain, human or otherwise. In other words, structurally, ANNs resemble the human brain in that they are complicated, with lots of simple elements in the network, but a closer look at the structure reveals dissimilarities as well.

Now consider the functional aspects of ANNs. The functioning of artificial neurons reflects what we knew about biological neurons around the mid-twentieth century: that neurons are either "firing" or not, resembling digital computers. Today, it seems that at least a small subset of neurons (maybe only a few million) display a more complex behavior, more akin to analog computers; that is, beyond whether the neuron is firing or not, the strength of the impulse it provides seems to matter. An experimental neuroscientist told me that neurons are not at all as well-behaved as they are represented as being. He observed at least two orders of magnitude of variation in responses to the same stimulus. While these are usually averaged when reported in academic journals, an average does not exist. All this means that a functioning ANN will be rather limited in comparison to the human brain.

If ANN architects managed to construct something like an artificial brain, some enthusiasts emphasize that as artificial neurons are faster than biological ones, the artificial brain should be better, or at least faster, than the biological one. However, here we face another assumption: that the artificial brain would produce an artificial mind. This may sound plausible, but it is just an assumption. What we know so far is that brain and mind are somehow connected, and particular thinking processes can be associated with activity in particular brain areas. We do not really understand how the brain and the mind are linked. The typical computer science analogy for cognition is that the brain is the hardware and the mind is the software – although the software is running on the hardware, hardware has never produced software. If the same part of my processor is active every time I write, it does not mean that that part of my processor writes the book.

Finally, recent research also suggests that the brain is not the only part of our biological setup that forms part of our cognitive system; our endocrine systems also seem to be part of it, and it would be unsurprising if we found in the coming years that our whole body is part of it. It would simply mean that the mind is fully "embodied." In other words, an artificial brain may or may not produce an artificial mind.

2.4 What Is AI, Then?

Aside from the three dominant types of AI described in this section, a few other types have been developed and used as independent systems or mixed with other types. The largest one not covered in detail here is Fuzzy Logic (FL); originally conceptualized by Lotfi Zadeh (1965), FL is used on its own a lot in engineering, as it makes control loops exceptionally effective. For instance, you can find it in the anti-lock braking system (ABS) of Volkswagen cars, in the washing cycle regulation of many washing machines (typically the pricier ones), etc. In AI, it is sometimes used in combination with ANN as well as symbolic expert systems. Genetic and evolutionary algorithms are other types that use random mutations that can produce better solutions using a suitably chosen fitness function. Genetic algorithms are well aligned with ANNs, and they can be used in both types of symbolic AI as well – although computer games are the only obvious example of this. These will not be expanded upon, as they do not represent different robust AI approaches, only variations on the types already introduced. Instead, based on the three AI types, we can now explain what counts as AI. The term *artificial intelligence* has two meanings. On the one hand, it refers to (artificially) intelligent machines and the ways of making them. On the other hand, AI is also a transdisciplinary field of study of these machines. AI gurus, such as Simon, often emphasized that studying AI involves studying the human mind. Therefore, the field of AI involves various branches of hard sciences and engineering, but beyond these also biology, psychology, and philosophy. In both uses of the term, AI is loosely defined as machines that can accomplish tasks that humans would accomplish through thinking. It is important to note here that this definition does not claim that the tasks are accomplished in the same ways as humans do them.

So how do we know that a machine thinks (in the same or a different sense than the human meaning of thinking)? How do we know whether it should be considered (artificially) intelligent? The first criterion, the Turing test, as proposed by Alan Turing (1950), is still the most popular today. The essence of the Turing test is that if we interact with an entity and are unable to figure out whether it is a person or a machine and it is, in fact, a machine, it means that the machine "thinks," and it should be considered intelligent. At first sight this sounds convincing; if the machine is not really thinking, we should be able to catch it out. Before unpacking the assumptions and implications of the test, let me ask this: Do you think that any machine (computer program) has passed the

Turing test so far? It is possible to claim that quite a few did. The first one was likely to have been Joseph Weizenbaum's (1966) ELIZA, followed by many other programs up to today's chatbots (such as Cleverbot: see Aron, 2011) and the most recent candidate, Eugene Goostman, the simulated 13-year-old Ukrainian boy (Warwick & Shah, 2016). This topic can be addressed in two steps: first in terms of the legitimacy of these "passes" and then by examining what it means that a machine passed the Turing test – if it did so legitimately.

Most programs passed the test with people who did not know that they were testing. The first experiment that was actually set up as a test was Eugene Goostman. Was this test legitimate? Well, it "fooled 33% of the untrained amateur judges" (Russell & Norvig, 2020). As a university teacher, I do not pass students at 33 percent – but there are greater problems as well; that is, having someone who is 13, from a country about which the testers do not know much, speaking English as a foreign language – well, the setup certainly worked in favor of the outcome. However, look at some example conversations (Aaronson, 2014) and make up your own mind – do you think this could possibly be a person? Personally, I tend to agree with Stuart Russell and Peter Norvig (2020), who say: "Perhaps the Turing test is really a test of human gullibility."

Having said all this, we can allow the possibility that an AI will at some point legitimately pass the Turing test. The question is: What then? Does passing the test really mean that the machine thinks in the sense in which we attribute this verb to humans? No, I do not think so. Let us have another look at the Turing test. Turing modeled his test on the "imitation game." In this game, you pretend to be someone else. You learn as much as you can about the other person and then you try to convince others that you are that person. If you learned your lesson well, you may succeed. Does this mean that you have miraculously become that other person? Of course not. The programs that passed the Turing test were designed with this purpose: to pass the test; to fool people into believing that they think, not to actually think.

Perhaps the most convincing argument against the Turing test comes from John Searle (1998: 11) in what is known as the *Chinese Room Argument*. The essence of the argument is the following: Assume that I do not speak Chinese, and I am in a room full of rulebooks, receiving messages in the form of Chinese symbols and looking up responses to those messages in the rulebooks. If the rulebooks are good, those outside the room, receiving the responses, would believe that the person responding understands Chinese – and they would be wrong; I did not suddenly learn Chinese. In the same way, passing the Turing test does not prove that the computer thinks, only that the program is good.

Of course, with these examples and arguments, it is not proven that machines cannot think, only that the usual evidence that they do is insufficient. So we are left to our respective beliefs, as there is no conclusive proof. While in this section the focus was on computers, Sections 3, 4, and 5 compare computers with humans along various dimensions, trying to establish what benefits of AI we can harvest and how. Do not forget: I am an AI enthusiast – I just see a different way to get the best out of it. But before getting to the next section, let me summarize a few takeaway points.

2.5 So What?

We need to be meticulous in discerning facts from beliefs regarding AI in order to avoid treating beliefs as facts. Here are a few facts:

- There is not just one type of AI. Although artificial neural networks (ANNs) dominate the AI landscape today, there are several types of AI. You can choose one or combine a few, as is often done in the best AI today (see the AlphaFold example in subsection 5.4), whatever suits your purpose.
- It looks like different things are difficult for humans and machines. Understanding prose is easy for humans, particularly native speakers. Proving a mathematical theorem, however, many find difficult, not to mention multiplying two six-digit numbers. In contrast, machines do the latter fast and effortlessly. A few specialized AI solutions were even able to prove some theorems, but understanding their meanings seems, at least for now, like a hopeless endeavor.
- Despite the claims of the thinking machine (also called wide AI and artificial general intelligence – AGI), so far, all forms of AI only deliver excellent performance in narrow, well-defined knowledge domains. Beyond those boundaries they are largely irrelevant. The rest is the promises, inferences, and hopes of some.

And now let me share a personal belief. Since the 1950s, we have witnessed a few waves of different application types dominating the AI landscape. Today, ANNs have nearly a monopoly. I believe that this is not the final word in AI. I think that the waves of various AI types will continue, and, like Davenport and O'Dell (2019), I believe that expert systems will be back once again. I am also confident that there will be a substantial shift towards hybrid AI, the combination of expert systems, ANN, and probably other forms of AI, including Fuzzy Logic and evolutionary computing.

3 Knowing

Logic is the beginning of wisdom ... not the end.

Spock[9]

This section delineates what knowledge means in the case of humans and in the case of machines, and how knowledge connects to other realms of the person or of the machine. This aspect of the analysis is primarily relevant to expert systems, which contain knowledge bases, although some AI specialists expect that ANNs would also infer some sort of knowledge about the world from their learning examples – but this is a topic for Section 4. My scholarly interest in knowing, learning, creating, and intuiting – particularly in the case of top experts – led me to interview 20 top scientists, including 17 Nobel Laureates. This study forms the background of this section and Sections 4 and 5 as well.

3.1 Explicit and Tacit

In order to easily make sense of the assertions made in this subsection, it is useful to use a more comprehensive picture of knowledge as a reference point; one that includes, besides scientific knowledge, other types as well, such as making coffee, writing a poem, enjoying the taste of strawberry, and so on. Just think of TV adverts claiming that "this detergent kills 99.7% of bacteria." This is why George Kelly (1955) asserts that "we are all scientists": It is not a job description; it is a worldview. Furthermore, we have to separate the notion of truth from the notion of knowledge. We have become accustomed to thinking that if we *know something*, it means that *it is true*. Kenneth Boulding (1966) argued that it is a significant epistemological problem that, in the English language, we cannot conceptualize knowledge simply as a mental content without assuming the truth of that content. This is a significant issue, as, for example, we know that the world is not flat, but nearly all engineering (with the exception of rocket design) works with that knowledge, and works well, as to make a car or a building we do not need to take into consideration that the Earth is shaped more like a ball. And if we wanted to be very precise, which would be necessary for truth, we would go from sphere to ellipsoid, then to a distorted ellipsoid, and end up inevitably with a shape called geoid, which loosely translates to "something like the Earth" ... if we get very precise about the shape of Earth, the only object (planet or other) in the category will be Earth itself.

The two problems seem to go together; that is, people prioritize scientific knowledge, as it is believed to be true. Some would even go so far as to argue

---

[9] *Star Trek VI: The Undiscovered Country* (1991): https://youtu.be/A4XPTmmvVow

that science is the only true knowledge. However, science and truth are actually in contradiction:

> It is one of the paradoxes of modern epistemology that we take science as the paradigm case of knowledge, yet insist upon a conception of wholly explicit truth. For science lives by discovery and ever further discovery; without the itch to solve problems, to follow hunches, to try out new and imprecise ideas, science would cease to exist. (Polányi, 1969: ix)

How we got to praise science over any other form of knowledge is unclear. Some claim that it is Aristotle's doing, but it is definitely not my reading of Aristotle; he certainly also praised *phrónēsis* (Ancient Greek: φρόνη ς, usually translated as either practical wisdom or practical virtue). However, even if one believes science to be superior to all other forms of knowledge, it does not make science the only form of knowledge. Furthermore, science also relies on aspects of knowledge that are not scientific. A few other aspects are explored in further detail later in this section and Section 4; for now, the focus is on the explicitness of knowledge.

Nonscientists tend to think of scientific knowledge as wholly explicit – and it is, once so well established that it is incorporated into handbooks. However, there is a long way to go to get there. As noted above with reference to truth, the production of scientific knowledge involves a great deal of tacit knowing (Polányi, 1966b). There is a myth of a "scientific method" producing scientific knowledge – the problem is that nobody knows what it is; as seen in my interviews, every great scientific result involved an intuitive insight (Dörfler & Ackermann, 2012; Dörfler & Eden, 2019). Intuiting belongs in the realm of tacit knowing: We know, but we do not really know how we know; it is a form of direct knowing (Dörfler & Stierand, 2017; Sinclair & Ashkanasy, 2005). What is essential to understand about tacit knowledge is that it is not simply knowledge that is not yet put into words; it *cannot* be put into words. Tacit knowledge is "unspoken and unspeakable" (Stierand, 2015). Why do I insist on this so much? Because there is no knowing without tacit knowing:

> While tacit knowledge can be possessed by itself, explicit knowledge must rely on being tacitly understood and applied. Hence all knowledge is either tacit or rooted in tacit knowledge. A wholly explicit knowledge is unthinkable. (Polányi, 1966a: 7)

This is perhaps the strongest assertion that Michael Polányi ever made against what many would like to believe about knowledge and science. Polányi went to great lengths and wrote a complete book just to show how any and all forms of knowing must be rooted in the tacit dimension, and he concluded: "tacit knowing is in fact the dominant principle of all knowledge, and that its rejection would, therefore, automatically involve the rejection of any knowledge whatever" (Polányi, 1959: 13).

CEOs, and managers in general, will have no problem appreciating tacit knowing; they are very well aware of the importance of "gut feel" in their decisions, their negotiations, and all areas of their work. The reason that it is crucial for us to understand the role of tacit knowing is that both types of symbolic AI – the symbolic reasoning systems and the expert systems – fully rely on explicit knowledge. This is similar to reducing a CEO's expertise to what can be written in an MBA handbook on decisions or strategizing. To be sure, it is important to read those books, and it is important to teach MBA students *about* decision making and *about* strategizing. The key word is *about*. We cannot teach deciding or strategizing; we can only teach *about* these. A management guru, Chris Argyris, asserted at an AoM conference that if we made decisions according to our MBA handbooks on decision making, we would never get out of bed, as by the time we were done with the decisions that we make along the way, it would be time to go to bed again.

For developing a symbolic reasoning system, the steps of problem-solving are obtained using the "thinking aloud" technique. While this approach can be very useful for understanding highly complex cognitive processes such as creativity or problem-solving better (Sowden et al., 2020), it is far from being sufficient for recreating these processes. When developing knowledge bases for expert systems, the knowledge engineer, little by little, teases out the knowledge from the experts (Baracskai & Velencei, 2002). Occasionally, a tiny part of tacit knowledge becomes explicit in these processes, and these are the celebrated moments of "knowledge discovery"; often the most valuable aspects of the knowledge engineering process. Even though expert systems are localized in very narrow domains of expertise, only a tiny fraction of the tacit knowledge of the expert is made explicit – if any. Mostly, knowledge engineering acquires and organizes what is already explicit about the problem domain. I would not hazard any percentages, but explicit knowledge is only a minuscule part of the expert's knowledge. Therefore, limiting AI to explicit knowledge would be sufficient to argue why computers cannot have real expertise. However, this only covers knowledge that we explicitly put into AI, not what it can learn on its own. That problem is addressed in Section 4; for now, it would be worthwhile to explore some additional aspects of knowledge and related realms, as these are in humans, in order to make a better delineation from a machine.

3.2 Personal Knowledge

One important feature of knowledge is that it is fundamentally personal. In some ways, this means that knowledge is necessarily subjective, although Polányi, in his original conceptualization, emphasizes that personal knowledge "transcends the disjunction between subjective and objective" (Polányi, 1962a: 316). In this sense, the notion of personal knowledge entails intentionality, drive, and passion, rather than simply enduring our feelings. In any case, we are talking about an instance of idiosyncrasy; that is, each person's personal knowledge is unique. This poses a major problem for any attempt to make knowledge bases (or any sort of knowledge representations) universal. In order to start unpacking this idiosyncrasy, I look at the characteristics of knowledge that I have observed by interviewing Nobel Laureates, but I also make links to everyday experiences that we all have.

The thinking of top scientists (Dörfler & Eden, 2019) – as well as that of the top experts in any profession, such as top chefs (Stierand & Dörfler, 2016) – is characterized by *intuitive leaps*. The problem with intuiting, in the context of AI, is that intuiting is nonalgorithmic. In a sense, we do not really know how intuiting works. It is usually described as a form of direct knowing that does not involve conscious sequential processing (Sinclair & Ashkanasy, 2005). Naturally, such a process cannot be captured using a thinking aloud technique. Intuitions (the outcomes of the process of intuiting) that have already happened can be incorporated into knowledge bases (and they frequently are); however, this does not help further intuitions appear. In short, we cannot get AI to reproduce intuiting, and if it did achieve that in some other way, we would not recognize it, as we do not have a model that describes the process of intuiting in sufficient detail. However, intuiting exists and constitutes an import-ant part of our thinking, even if the scientific knowledge of it is limited (Dörfler & Bas, 2020a). How important are intuitions? Based on my interviews with the Nobel Laureates, I would risk the assertion that not a single significant research result seems to have been achieved without intuition playing a major role in the process.

Another aspect of personal knowledge is knowing *harmony and beauty*. We can admire the beauty of a rainbow, and it does not even matter whether we understand the optical effect that produces it; it may be just the consequence of a prism, but it is still beautiful. Scientists, chefs, and other top experts make great use of such knowledge when creating new things, regardless of whether it is a painting, a new dish, or a new scientific idea (cf. Wilczek, 2015). Perhaps the best-known example from science is that of James Clark Maxwell and his famous equations that describe electromagnetism. He deduced the initial form of his equations, taking into consideration all knowledge from theoretical and experimental physics. Then he looked at the equations, said that they were not beautiful, and added a component. At the time, the added component made only an infinitesimal difference, so it was impossible to tell which version was right. However, once the measurements were refined, it was found that the component that Maxwell added to make the equations beautiful is necessary, as the equations are incorrect otherwise. We all observe what we see as beautiful when creating something; for instance, this was how I envisaged the structure of this book.

Analogical thinking is about having mental models, analogous to reality, that we can work with. Perhaps the most famous example from science is the case of Nikola Tesla, who created his machines in his mind, modified them there, fixed any malfunctions, and once they worked perfectly in his mind, he built them in reality and they also worked perfectly (Tesla, 1919: 11–12). The only time when Tesla had to make blueprints was when he filed a patent – for his work, this was unnecessary. Analogical thinking corresponds to what in the human mind is called an analogical representational system (Rumelhart & Norman, 1988). We all have these, although not many of us are as sharply tuned as Tesla. If you think of a house in which you have lived, you can count the windows, go around it in your mind, noticing the neighbor's fence, and so forth. If you think about your most recent hot breakfast, you will recall not only the visuality but also the smell of the eggs, the sound of the cutlery, and all the flavors. All this is to say that the analogical representational system is multisensory and holistic, and the facts we can line up just do not do the job.

Finally, I have observed something that I call *seeing the essence*. The first half of it is pretty trivial with reference to top experts: They can see the "big picture." This means that they understand the whole situation, together with the context, as one, as well as all the connections of this whole to anything else it may be connected to. They are also exceptionally good at seeing the details, and they can almost instantaneously switch between the big picture and the detail. Furthermore, they also know (intuitively) the relationship between any of the details and the whole. This is remarkable, as the details do not make the whole, as we know from cybernetics. Mistakenly, it is often said that the whole is *more* than the mere sum of the parts – in fact, the whole is *something different* from the sum of its parts. Just think of a couple, where you knew both members from before. They, as a couple, are something different from the two individuals. Moreover, each member is different as part of the couple than on her/his own. In other words, the whole determines the parts as much as the parts constitute the whole. This is why complex systems cannot be decomposed and put back together. Therefore, it is incredible that top experts can "see" what happens to the big picture if we change a particular detail. It is even more impressive that if they want to change the big picture in a particular way (e.g. to fix it), they know which detail to change and how. I consider this to be evidence of the nonlinear nature of thinking – AI is notoriously linear. This description resonates with Iain McGilchrist's (2019) *The Master and His Emissary* model, where the Master, corresponding to the right brain, is in charge of the big picture, while the Emissary, corresponding to the left brain, deals with the details and is subordinate to the Master – unfortunately, recently in the Western world we have tended to favor the Emissary and neglect the Master, and in AI we can see the same tendency.

The focus is on the highest level of mastery in this subsection because the examined characteristics can be particularly well observed in the case of top experts, and these are not minor things that only exist at a low level of expertise; these are essential for the high performance of human thinking. In fact, many assume that knowledge becomes more abstract with the increase of expertise, as it makes sense that if more and more knowledge is accumulated, it will be more general, and more general seems to be more abstract. In fact, the Dreyfus brothers, Hubert and Stuart (1986), have shown that knowledge is most abstract at the novice level, as the novice cannot connect the newly learned with real-life experience. With the increase of mastery, knowledge becomes more and more concrete. Furthermore, intuition becomes more and more dominant with the increase of mastery (Dörfler et al., 2009; Dreyfus & Dreyfus, 1986; Simon, 1996). This also means that we cannot easily make parallels between what is difficult or easy in the case of the human mind and AI. Newell and Simon judged the job for which they built the Logic Theorist complex because it is taught at college level (Newell et al., 1963). While proving mathematical theorems is quite difficult for humans, a relatively simple AI did it, while understanding the meaning of a text – which is effortless to most humans – seems to present a hard barrier for AI.

3.3 Knowledge Is Not Alone

Besides the many aspects of personal knowledge that do not seem to be amenable to replication or emulation by AI, it is also important to see how knowledge relates to other aspects of our being. The three most important aspects here are feelings, emotions, and values (the values are discussed in more detail in Section 6).

Feelings seem to get in the way of rational thought. When we are hungry, we cannot pay attention. If we are afraid of falling, we do not try to jump. It may seem that feelings are not to the advantage of humans in comparison to AI. The question is not whether feelings are good or bad; simply that they contribute to making humans different. Of course, humans can use their knowledge to temporarily override their feelings, but only temporarily. Feelings are closely linked to our instincts and therefore to fundamental needs (Dörfler & Szendrey, 2008). We feel hunger, thirst, desire for sex, fear of death, longing for the company of other people, etc. We can postpone any of these for some time, but eventually we must give in to our feelings; we must eat, sleep, get away from the source of fear, and so on. However, the ability to control our feelings is of paramount importance. Some biologists, like von Bertalanffy (1981), and some psychologists, like Fromm (1942), go so far as to suggest that this is one of the essential features of being human in comparison to animals. In comparison with AI, not having feelings in the first place does not compare to having feelings and being able to free ourselves from their control and deal with them on our own terms.

In contrast to feelings, *emotions* are located "higher" than knowledge in the sense that emotions can overpower knowledge, similarly to how knowledge overpowers feelings. The philosopher David Hume (1739: 415) asserted that "Reason is, and ought only to be the slave of the passions, and can never pretend to any other office than to serve and obey them." In this line of thought, humans decide what they want on the basis of emotions and use reason to figure out how to achieve it. More recently, Antonio Damasio (1995) has worked with a patient he refers to as Elliot, who lost his emotional center in an accident; that is, he could not experience any emotions. Although all his mental faculties were working flawlessly, he lost his job, became socially awkward, and could not deliver in any human context that was previously his natural setting. He was able to do never-ending mathematical calculations correctly, but he could not draw a picture. He could argue endlessly for one or another decision alternative (e.g. arranging the next appointment with Damasio) but could not make a choice. This extensive study provides substantial evidence for the indispensability of emotions for human decisions.

Values come into play when we do something because we believe that it is the right thing to do, not in order to achieve a goal. Because of certain values that we hold, we can transcend our own self-interest and act irrespectively of, or even contrary to, what we want, even though we have complete clarity regarding what we want. A father going on a holiday with his daughter may choose the seaside because she likes it, although he would prefer mountains. Of course, this is a trivial example, but countless decisions of parents, children, lovers, and friends belong here. Values may also come from society or religion or political parties or companies or any sort of organization, so we do what is socially acceptable or what the particular sacred documents or teacher or politician or manager says is the right thing to do. The really tricky thing about values is that we have them in a messy system rather than a neatly organized linear list, and we inherit some from our families and some from peer groups, schools, societies, etc. However, we do not just adopt them; we also adapt them, create new ones from scratch, combine existing ones, and throw away those with which we do not align any more. As we relate to all these social formations, James March (1994) says that the first question we ask should always be the Don Quixotean "who am I?", and that we take all sorts of things into consideration that have nothing to do with the decision at hand in the first place, such as other projects we need time for or how it will affect someone who is our partner on a different project, and there argues that decisions happen there rather than being made in organizations (Dörfler, 2021).

So, as a departure from rational decisions, we sometimes give in to our feelings, sometimes our emotions dominate, and sometimes we follow particular values. Of course, it would be possible to program one or more of these, only that is not how we obtain them and, just like with knowledge, much of what is there is in the tacit dimension. Most AI researchers do not overlook the problem of feelings, emotions, and values, but they usually dismiss it either by saying that "we should first get the knowledge stuff sorted, and then we'll get the rest done," or they suggest that AI will probably learn these together with knowledge, and if not, then it is probably not worth dealing with them. There is, however, the curious case of Minsky, who was a true believer in AGI and a very fine thinker.

Minsky (2006) reversed Searle's Chinese Room Argument, envisaging a hypothetical "zombie machine." The zombie machine was supposed to be identical to humans in appearance and, if it got hurt – for example, injured a leg – it would complain about the pain. Of course, the complaint is its programming; if the programming were good, what we would see in its response to the pain would be indistinguishable from a human with a pain in their leg. Could we still claim that the zombie machine does not feel pain? In the logic of the Chinese Room Argument, we can do that. However, Minsky then turns it around again to get to the original point he wanted to make: If we cannot distinguish the zombie machine from a human being and we can claim that the zombie machine does not feel pain, can we really claim that the human being feels pain? Of course, generally we cannot, and we have all seen humans pretending to feel pain – for instance, in a football game. However, this score of wits is not really what Minsky was after. He fully realized that emotions are of paramount importance for intelligence, human or otherwise, which is why he said:

> The question is not whether intelligent machines can have any emotions, but whether machines can be intelligent without any emotions. I suspect that once we give machines the ability to alter their own abilities we'll have to provide them with all sorts of complex checks and balances. It is probably no accident that the term "machinelike" has come to have two opposite connotations. One means completely unconcerned, unfeeling, and emotionless, devoid of any interest. The other means being implacably committed to some single cause. Thus each suggests not only inhumanity, but also some stupidity. Too much commitment leads to doing only one single thing; too little concern produces aimless wandering. (Minsky, 1988: 163)

3.4 The Achievement of Meaning

Following his early encounter with the Logic Theorist (subsection 2.1), Feigenbaum undertook a project called Elementary Perceiver and Memorizer (EPAM), which was intended to be a model of human cognition. The story of EPAM started in September 1956 (Feigenbaum, 2006: 7:30), just as Feigenbaum returned from his summer holiday. Simon pointed out to him an article on human learning in a then-recent issue of the *Scientific American*. The article was concerned with verbal learning; specifically with memorizing meaningless lists of random words. Simon was happy with the article, as it included data about what he labeled "elementary learning," as it the simplest possible instance within the scope of human learning. The EPAM was extremely successful. Building on the assumption that as there is no meaning attached, the observed outcome (better recalling the beginnings and ends of the lists) must have had something to do with memory structures. Simon wanted a computer model that offered an explanation, including a quantitative prediction of the experimental outcomes. The EPAM did, and it became Feigenbaum's PhD dissertation topic (Feigenbaum & Simon, 1984; Simon & Feigenbaum, 1964). The really important point here is that at that time, meaning was not part of the deal; it was all about memory structures. I do not think that any projection into the realm of meaning based on memory structures only is sensible, as we cannot derive meaning by just adding more stuff with no meaning.

It seems that in order to figure out what AI can and cannot do, whether it can be intelligent in the same sense as humans are, and whether it can think, it is important to get a better grip on the notion of meaning. First, I want to provide some substance for my previous assertion that adding more stuff with no meaning cannot produce meaning. The easiest evidence to observe for the assertion that adding more stuff with no meaning cannot produce meaning comes from language. Noam Chomsky (1957) showed that syntactic structures are independent of semantics, meaning that grammar and the structure of sentences can be understood without any reference to meanings whatsoever. This suggests that memory structures could be similar, and therefore studying memory structures may not be informative regarding the meaning. As Polányi argued, this is a multi-level system in which the higher level does not contradict the lower level, but it also cannot be derived from that lower level; rather, there are higher-level principles that operate in the space left open by the lower-level principles. In Polányi's words: "You cannot derive a vocabulary from phonetics; you cannot derive grammar from a vocabulary; a correct use of grammar does not account for good style; and a good style does not provide the content of a piece of prose" (Polányi, 1966a: 16).

Then again, it is also possible that the memory structures are based on meaning. Indeed, the dominant view in cognitive psychology is that we store propositional knowledge in the form of semantic networks in the mind (Rumelhart & Norman, 1988). There are many debates on how these semantic networks are constructed; obviously, they are based on the meanings of the concepts, each concept could be described with a number of semantic attributes, there would be links between the concepts, and these links would also have their semantic attributes. For instance, the concept of the ball would be linked to all the spherical shapes that we have in our mind and also with the abstract notion of being spherical, as well as with many other objects, for example, with a table. This latter relationship should also have a qualifier that explains that a ball can be on the top of the table – but it also perhaps should not be there. One may not have a link between a ball and a window unless one has seen a ball breaking a window or has imagined the same. This is a speculative model, and it sounds fairly plausible, even though it is predominantly based on assumptions. What the experimental work has shown is that these webs of concepts we may have in our minds are weird; as Douglas Hofstadter (1979) says, they feature "strange loops" that may connect several levels of a hierarchical system and involve paradoxes and self-reference. For example, it has been established how long it takes for the mind to move from one concept to another one to which it is directly connected. Based on this, it was figured that the dolphin–fish connection should be four units, following the pattern dolphin–cetacean–mammal–vertebrate–fish. Instead, it has been found that for most people it is one unit; that is, we seem to have a "not fish" concept directly connected to the concept of dolphin (cf. Mérő, 1990). This is just one trivial example of how the well-structured hierarchy breaks down, suggesting that if we indeed have semantic networks in our minds, they are anything but well-structured.

There are two people who contributed a great deal to AI development, who took a stand on what I think of as meaning. The first one is Terry Winograd, whose SHRDLU[10] project was the first natural language processing (NLP) program and the predecessor of all NLP and speech recognition programs today. However, there was a turn in Winograd's work, and he became a philosopher.

> What I came to realize is that the success of the communication depends on the real intelligence on the part of the listener, and that there are many other ways of communicating with a computer that can be more effective, given that it doesn't have the intelligence. At that point, I shifted my view away from what would be thought of as artificial intelligence to the broader question, "How do you want to interact with a computer?" Then I got interested in what makes interactions with computers work well or fail and what makes them fluent. That's been the direction of my work.
>
> (Moggridge, 2007: 457)

Another person who left a lasting mark in the field of AI worth mentioning here is Weizenbaum. Having created the first software that passed the Turing test (see ELIZA in subsection 2.4), Weizenbaum concluded that computers have a problem with the notion of meaning. In fact, Hubert Dreyfus praises this achievement as the triumph of the mind over machine: "Weizenbaum set out to show just how much apparent intelligence one could get a computer to exhibit without giving it 'any semantic endowment at all,' thereby reducing Minsky's method to absurdity" (Dreyfus & Dreyfus, 1986: 71).

We have to admit that, at least for now, we have nothing that resembles the achievement of meaning in AI – at least not in the same sense as meaning in the human mind. Theodore Roszak, a sociologist of information systems (IS) who wrote what I think of as the best book so far written about IS, says:

> The prospect of machine interpretation is not only whimsical; it is absurd. Interpretation belongs solely to a living mind in exactly the same way that birth belongs solely to a living body. Disconnected from a mind, "interpretation" becomes what "birth" becomes when it does not refer to a body: a metaphor. (Roszak, 1986: 131)

3.5 So What?

Scientific knowledge is not the only type of knowledge, and knowledge is not necessarily true. One of the essential criteria of a good scientist is to be

---

[10] SHRDLU is curiously not an acronym; it is the arrangement of keys on the Linotype Machine (typesetting machine from the pre-digital era of printing) that follows the descending order of usage frequency in English.

sufficiently open-minded to allow the possibility of being wrong. In addition, knowledge comes in various shapes and forms, and only the simple explicit facts are something that AI can put up with. So here are a few critical facts:

- A crucial problem with modeling is that we can only model something of which we know the original. Although we have all experienced understanding, we do not understand understanding and cannot model it.
- Any knowledge representation means restricting knowledge to explicit knowledge. Everyone in the field of AI knows this. What they may not know is that any meaningful knowledge is unimaginable without tacit knowing.
- Knowledge does not exist alone. Amongst others, our feelings, emotions, and values interact with our knowledge. Be aware of siding too quickly with those who argue that these are just imperfections preventing the perfect rational thought. Feelings, emotions, and values seem to make precious contributions to our lives, conducting business, and science itself. When interviewing Nobel Laureates, a common thread connecting all of them was their deep love of their respective fields of study.

On a personal note, I believe that the most valuable aspects of human knowledge are precisely those that cannot be replicated or emulated in AI. These aspects include intuition, the sense of beauty, metaphors, and where knowledge intersects with other realms, such as feelings, emotions, and values. Furthermore, human knowledge is sensory-based (Bas et al., 2022), meaning that we learn from our experiences. Let us use AI to handle the boring facts while we focus on the more exciting things. However, for this to happen, we need to change our educational system to focus on what humans are good at rather than on what AI can do.

4 Learning

Personally, I am always ready to learn, although I do not always like being taught.
Winston Churchill[11]

This section contrasts machine with human learning. In order to do this, as in Section 3, I make use of my experience interviewing Nobel Laureates. We humans all learn in the ways I describe here, but it is perhaps easier to observe the patterns in the cases of those who have achieved the highest level of mastery. It has fascinated me for most of my life how we can learn anything at all.

4.1 Talent and Inspiration

First, I want to look into some antecedents of learning. We can all tell our own stories regarding what we were particularly good and bad at learning. For me, mathematics and physics never presented a problem. History, on the other hand, was a serious problem. Then, in high school, I got an excellent history teacher, and history was not a problem any longer. So it seems to me that there are two things that together have an enormous impact on how we learn: whether we have the talent and how we feel about it.

What does it mean to be talented at something? Without getting too deep into cognitive psychology, we simply seem to be more disposed to explore certain domains than others, and we learn more rapidly in these areas (Gardner, 1995). We call this talent or – with a beautiful English word – a gift. It is a gift, as we have not earned it – but what does it mean to be more disposed? Why do we learn more rapidly? My answer to this is not the official standpoint of cognitive psychology, as it is a debated area. Furthermore, this answer does not originate from cognitive psychology literature; it is coming from a high school mathematics teacher who identified a number of pupils who later became exceptional mathematicians. She said that it was as if these kids already had all the mathematical structures in their minds, and she only needed to label those structures. I am not advocating the obsolete view of innate knowledge of a domain, but to me, this sounds like the everyday knowledge of these kids being organized in similar ways to the knowledge in the domain in which they are talented. Think of an area in which you learned quickly: It usually feels like play rather than work; it is fun; you seek more and more challenging tasks, and it does not feel like you are learning at all. It feels as if you only need to be shown, then you understand, and then it just naturally works. I have been on the other side as well: I learned a few chords on a guitar and, years later, it was still all

---

[11] 1952, November 4, Hansard, United Kingdom Parliament, Commons, Speaking: The Prime Minister Winston Churchill, HC Deb 04, volume 507, cc7-134. http://hansard .millbanksystems.com/commons/1952/nov/04/debate-on-the-address

I knew. I showed all I knew to someone who was obviously talented at music. It took him literally hours to become better than I was, and a week later he could play anything by ear. There is a tendency to diminish the role of talent in some of the literature on expertise development (Ericsson & Charness, 1994); in simple terms, as the journalists often say about great achievements, it was 10 percent talent and 90 percent hard work. To me this is nonsense. It would seem that extraordinary achievement always comes from the combination of 100 percent talent and 100 percent hard work. But the extraordinary (Dörfler & Stierand, 2019) is not the topic of this book, so I resist getting more into the details about particularly gifted humans. What is important is that we are all more talented in some areas than in others, and this human dependence on talent is often portrayed as a disadvantage in comparison with AI. AI does not need talent. I have never seen it spelled out, but my impression is often that "AI is talented at everything" is implied. If it is even possible to figure out what talent means in the context of AI, I would certainly agree that AI is *equally* talented in any domain, which is the same as saying that AI is not talented at anything. I could support the latter variant with the observation that one of the signs of talent is that intuition in the domain of the talent seems to start working when the level of expertise does not warrant that it should – and, as previously argued, there is nothing to suggest that intuition in AI would be possible.

Besides the domain we are learning in, it also seems to make a huge difference who is doing the teaching. Of course, it is not as simple as some teachers are good and some are bad. This is also true, but not all good teachers are equally good for all the good learners. I had an undergraduate student many years ago to whom I said that she should pursue a PhD, as she was excellent, but not with me. I could not explain why; I just intuitively knew that we were not a good match. We were in each other's proximity for the next few years, and she agreed when she saw how I worked with my PhD students that she could not have worked with me. So there are always several different ways to learn something, and some ways will suit us more than others. It may also happen that in different stages of our learning we need to pursue different learning styles. There is nothing like this in AI; there is only one learning style, and I will unpack its limitations in the next subsection.

However, before that, it is important to address the notion of inspiration observed with the interviewed Nobel Laureates. There was one huge inspiration in their lives, something that made them decide what they wanted to become, one great inspirational teacher. These great inspirational teachers seem to be extremely few; all but one of the physics Nobel Laureates interviewed were inspired either by Richard Feynman or by Enrico Fermi (Dörfler & Eden, 2017). There are a few such great changes in our learning, signified by the notion of "threshold concepts" (Meyer et al., 2010). Threshold concepts also signify that learning is not a simple cumulative exercise; apart from adding further knowledge, our learning involves extending the meaning of already learned concepts, reinterpreting concepts, and removing concepts either as they are superseded by better ones or simply as we realize that they are wrong (usually we do not forget them; we remember that they are wrong for us). So learning is a delicate interplay of learning and unlearning, which happens in a complex system where things (knowledge items) are not simply additive, as they interact with each other. Occasionally, during the learning process, we achieve a deeper understanding, in which many elements of our preexisting knowledge, and perhaps some new knowledge elements, arrange themselves into a complex pattern. In cognitive psychology, such transformational learning experiences are described as the formation of a meta-schema, and this phenomenon roughly corresponds to threshold concepts (cf. Dörfler, 2010). AI certainly does not feature such transformational learning events; its learning seems to follow the pyramid model (the new always builds on the acceptance of all the old). We humans would not get very far if we learned only in that way.

4.2 Beyond Skinner's Rats

At a September 2017 New Scientist Live event in London, Demis Hassabis, the founder and CEO of DeepMind, made two assertions: One of these is relevant here, while the second one will be addressed in Section 5. The first assertion was about the learning algorithms of DeepMind, namely that "DeepMind learns like people do – through reinforcement learning." Let me unpack what this means.

There was a historic period in the discipline of psychology, more or less in the first half of the twentieth century, usually referred to as "behaviorist psychology,"[12] when reinforcement learning was seen as the only way of learning. The name reveals that the focus is on the behavior rather than on what happens in the mind. In fact, this approach to psychology considered the mind to be a "black box," meaning that it became a discipline that denied its own research topic – a veritable "dark ages" of psychology. At the heart of the reinforcement learning approach is the so-called stimulus-response (S-R) model; we can observe behavior by examining the stimulus received by the entity (human, animal, machine) and the response it provides. Learning in this setup happens in a variant of reinforcement learning, in which we reward the preferred responses and/or punish the nonpreferred ones. If the entity is capable

---

[12] Not to be confused with behavioral psychology, which is the psychology of behavior, examining how environment shapes behavior, how the mind responds to the environment through behavior, and similar, and which is a perfectly legitimate contemporary branch of psychology – it does not reduce the mind to the behavior.

of learning, sooner or later it will always respond with the rewarded (or nonpunished) behavior. There was productivity in this framework; this was how Ivan Pavlov (1927) got to understand the Pavlovian reflexes and Burrhus Skinner (1950) trained his rats to press a pedal when they were hungry.[13] Although operant conditioning and other variants of reinforcement learning work well on rats, it is questionable if that is the way humans learn.[14]

It was certainly sensible for Turing (1950) to consider reinforcement learning at the time. However, psychology has come a long way since its "dark ages"; today we know that there is very little we learn through reinforcement learning. Of course, there are a few things that humans learn this way – for example, a child quickly learns not to touch a hot stove. However, we also learn from stories (told or written), observe others and imitate them, commit to master–apprentice relationships, invent new ways and educate ourselves about them, etc. Reinforcement learning covers only a tiny part of our learning. People can be conditioned as well, only most of us do not like to be conditioned – and there is so much more we do when we learn.

The same teaching material can be acquired in several different ways, particularly if we are not dealing with knowledge at an exceptionally high level of complexity. For instance, in university-level mathematics, some prefer to read abstract explanations, some prefer lectures delivered in similarly abstract ways, and others will only be interested in how the abstract things are implemented in problem-solving, and they usually practice solving problems to eventually get to the more abstract and generic principles. I have even met some who learned particularly well by writing down theorems and then the proofs, but this is all well-articulated and not too complex knowledge.

Perhaps the most complex form of learning takes place in *master–apprentice relationships*. Interestingly, we do not really know how the master–apprentice relationship works. What we do know is that it seems to be the only way of transferring tacit knowledge and that all who achieved the highest level of mastery, including the Nobel Laureates I have interviewed, did go through some form of master–apprentice relationship: "the methods of scientific inquiry cannot be explicitly formulated and hence can be transmitted only in the same way as an art, by the affiliation of apprentices to a master" (Polányi, 1969: 66).

A casual observer would say that the apprentice imitates the master. However, this is not simple imitation; this is what Polányi (1946: 29–30) calls

---

[13] I really like a caricature in which two rats in the Skinner box have a conversation about how well they have trained the experimenter – they only need to press a pedal and the experimenter brings the cheese.

[14] A brilliant and highly entertaining book on the topic is Daniel Keyes' (1966) *Flowers for Algernon*.

"intelligent imitation." In contrast to the parrot-like mindless copying, in intelligent imitation we learn in an adaptive way and can alter what we have learned, develop it further, and so forth. This is how we learn, for instance, our native language, and we can eventually become better at using this language than our parents and teachers, from whom we have learned it. This resembles how an apprentice can, eventually, surpass the master.

There is a paradox at the core of the master–apprentice relationship. The apprentice should imitate the master, as it is the master who knows. At the same time, it is wrong to imitate the master, as the apprentice who does that can only become a pale copy of the master. It is this very paradox, however, that hardens the apprentice. There is a struggle, from which the apprentice may emerge as a new master – a vastly improved version of themselves – rather than becoming a poor replica of the master. A part of this learning happens at a meta level, meaning that through examples, the masters demonstrate not only how things are done but also how unique they are on their own grounds. *If, and only if,* the apprentice is gifted and inspired, this uniqueness is understood and felt, and thus the apprentice may become "upgraded" to a more advanced version. As a purely intellectual exercise, the master–apprentice relationship will not work. It requires emotions as much as thinking; beliefs and the courage to transcend what is are essential. This is an ancient form of learning; just think about Socrates and his disciples in the Agora or the artist workshops in which Leonardo or Michelangelo were apprentices. Unfortunately, due to their asymmetry and because they take a long time, master–apprentice relationships are not very popular today. I argue and plead in each talk I give, and everything I write, to preserve and treasure this unique way of learning.

In their book *Working Knowledge*, Thomas Davenport and Larry Prusak (2000) tell the story of a satellite photo analyst who was reputed to be the best in the world. As he was nearing retirement, the major oil company for which he worked hired an expert system developer to codify this unique expertise (Davenport & Prusak, 2000: 84). Leaving the reader hanging with a half-answer that the expert system was a failure, the actual catharsis of the story is only provided 11 pages later:

> The long process of trying to extract and understand the expert's knowledge served as an apprenticeship. Having extensive conversations, looking at photographs together, asking questions, and seeking clarifications taught the consultant a new skill. When the project ended, the expert system was useless, but the system designer was said to be the second best analyzer of aerial photographs in the world! (Davenport & Prusak, 2000: 95)

4.3 Indwelling

Like so many ideas about knowledge and learning, indwelling was also conceptualized by Polányi (1962b). He borrowed the concept from those who used it to explain connoisseurship in arts; that is, that we can only know arts through indwelling, by projecting ourselves into the object of perception. Polányi (1962b) extends the notion to everything experiential and further to the whole domain of tacit knowing: *"We* pour ourselves out into them and assimilate them as parts of our own existence" (Polányi, 1962a: 61).

Most of us can easily understand how chefs feel about their knives, for example, as if they were part of their body. It is a little bit more difficult to imagine how fighter pilots might feel about their jets as part of their bodies or how an astrophysicist may dwell in "a galaxy far, far away" ... it is also really obscure to imagine a theoretical physicist dwelling in a quark-level symmetry or asymmetry, or a mathematician dwelling in an abstract topology. Yet their reports are very much like those of more hands-on professions; in this sense, we can think of indwelling as a more general concept of the embodiment of knowing (Dörfler & Stierand, 2018). This is an incredibly important aspect of learning and signifies the importance of experiential learning; however, dwelling in the subject of learning is only one aspect of indwelling that is relevant for learning.

Another important aspect of indwelling concerns other people. This is possibly why inspirational teachers are so important – but there is no specific evidence for that. What is clearer is how indwelling works in master–apprentice relationships. Apprentices, at the start of the process, do not reach the level of mastery where they can easily dwell in their subject of interest. However, they can dwell in their masters, and their masters dwell in the discipline, which is how the apprentices get to dwell in the discipline through their masters. We can call this *shared indwelling*. Apart from the traditional master–apprentice relationship described in the previous subsection, this is very observable in the "wandering apprentices," where the disciple goes from one master to another. Possibly it is not even so much the particular aspects of knowledge that dictate this; it could be the different aspects of indwelling. The third type of master–apprentice relationship that we identified we named (together with Eric Wieschaus, one of the interviewees) "mutual apprenticing" (Dörfler & Eden, 2017). It takes two people who are already very good but not quite "grandmasters"[15] yet, who meet at the right time and become one another's apprentice and master. An example of mutual apprenticing is Daniel Kahneman and Amos Tversky, who were described by others as "one mind being located in

---

[15] A term borrowed from chess to describe the highest level of expertise (Dörfler et al., 2009).

two people." We have also observed the shared mind phenomenon in communities of practice (CoPs), where we have named it "thinking together" (Pyrko et al., 2017), and found it to be the single most essential ingredient of CoPs. We have described it as "interlocked indwelling": "indwelling is interlocked on the same cue, they can guide each other through their understanding of a mutually recognized real-life problem, and in this way they indirectly "share" tacit knowledge" (Pyrko et al., 2017: 390).

It is perhaps interesting to note that the initial conceptualization of CoPs by Jeane Lave and Etienne Wenger (1991) was the result of studying master–apprentice relationships. What the CoP concept adds here is that the previous instances of people dwelling in each other only involved two people at a time (although in the case of wandering apprentices, this was not always the same two people), but in CoPs the individuals also dwell in the community. Perhaps it is not too surprising, then, that the fourth type of master–apprentice relationship, which we named "hot spot" (using the term suggested by Roy Glauber, one of the interviewees), is a kind of super-performing CoP. It is important to see that in the process of learning, and often in the process of performing, knowledge transcends the personal, which is why it is good to talk about transpersonal knowing processes as well. The significance of indwelling in all these forms of learning is the experiential aspect, which is not limited to the touchable world but may invoke the complete scope of the discipline, with all its distant and possibly abstract dimensions – and yet it is still a form of experience (cf. Bas et al., 2022). This is also important because it links back to the experiential nature of the threshold concepts; in a sense, transformational learning requires experiencing as well as the ability to reflect on these experiences (cf. Kahneman, 2011).

It is useful to stop for a moment and think about simulations here. When I was an MBA student, my class was shown a business simulation game. At the end of the exercise, I noted that all those who performed well were PhD students with zero organizational experience, while those who delivered the poorest performance in the game were experienced and highly regarded CEOs. What happened? The simulation could only perform what the programmers of the game could imagine about business – it was nonsense. However, this is true for any simulation. In some cases, the simulation can be pretty much the same as the real thing; think about a game of chess or Go. In other cases, such as marriage or politics or running a business, it is nothing alike. These extremes are relatively easy to identify, but to which end is a self-driving car closer? You will find similar examples in any organization.

4.4 Common Sense

There is something most AI researchers, from both the weak and the strong AI paradigm,[16] agree on: What is missing to create real AI, a real thinking machine, is a model of common sense. I read this first in Minsky (strong AI), and I (weak AI) fully agree with it. Where we have a difference of opinion is about how big a task that is; strong AI supporters think that it is just another step to figure out, while those in the weak AI paradigm think that it is impossible. So what is this common sense that is a source of such confusion and possibly the key to understanding what AI will ever be able to do?

Common sense is that taken-for-granted aspect of everyday knowledge that we seem to use all the time, regardless of whether we are dealing with highly specialized work or issues of private life. We usually do not even think of it as knowledge, yet without it, all knowledge seems to be impossible. Although it is not worth getting into a precise definition, all interpretations of common sense include a reference to sound judgment and also to the use of sensory perceptions and sensible thought processes. In everyday language, it also features the absence of explanation, which is considered unnecessary due to its triviality. Of course, if we actually try to explain something in the realm of common sense, we often find that the explanation may be far from trivial. Importantly, common sense is always concerned with the real world – the "practical" – and never with abstract philosophizing, which is why it is also quite difficult to philosophize about it.

While many things about common sense seem to be trivial, common sense itself is very far from trivial. It seems to involve a notion of generic agreement, yet it seems to be differently structured in different people's minds. So it seems that common sense is very personal, even if there are many outcomes that people agree about. Furthermore, people agree about it within more or less narrow communities. If we look at cultural differences between nations or regions or even within organizations, we will find that their common sense(s) can be quite different. What "goes without saying" here may be dictated very differently by another common sense somewhere else. Therefore, common sense is personal as well as transpersonal, and it is embedded in and dependent on context.

> Common sense is not a simple thing. Instead, it is an immense society of hard-earned practical ideas – of multitudes of life-learned rules and exceptions, dispositions and tendencies, balances and checks. If common sense is so diverse and intricate, what makes it seem so obvious and natural? This illusion of simplicity comes from losing touch with what happened during

---

[16] The distinction between strong and weak AI was introduced by John Searle (1980: 417); in the weak AI paradigm, AI is seen as a very useful and powerful tool, while the strong AI paradigm postulates AI as a mind on its own, at least as a desirable and achievable outcome.

infancy ... when we try to speak of them in later life, we find ourselves with little more to say than "I don't know." (Minsky, 1988: 22)

Of course, the intent is not to crack the problem of common sense as a sidebar in this book. But it is useful to try to figure out what it means for AI. If we contrast common sense with specialist knowledge, the successes of AI are all in the specialist category, typically in narrow domains of expertise. In those, we have seen AI outperform top experts in some areas (see more in Section 5) and deliver a performance on a par with a medium level of expertise in others. I am with Minsky here again: "Why is it easier to program what experts do than what children do?" (Minsky, 1988: 72).

This further makes me ask: What sort of knowledge level corresponds to common sense? It is estimated that most of our common sense is around the expert level,[17] as, for instance, speaking in our native language or handling everyday situations (Mérő, 1990: 122). Of course, if one is a writer, the native language is also an area of mastery, so it can be higher – but not for most of us.

We have very limited experience with AI in the area of common sense. There have been several attempts to develop artificial common sense, one of the best known being the "CYC knowledge base."[18] The CYC is probably the largest knowledge base ever produced, comprising "millions of facts, beliefs, and other bits of knowledge" (Feigenbaum, 1992: 17), contributed to by thousands of people. Having started in 1986, it appears to be the longest-running knowledge-based system project – it is still alive today, yet it still does not produce common sense. In fact, all the attempts to model common sense have remained futile so far, and none shows any progress that I would judge promising. In my view, we cannot develop artificial common sense, as we cannot acquire it from a single person, as it would take an unimaginably long time, and we cannot acquire it from multiple people due to the personal, transpersonal, sensory, and contextual nature of common sense. Perhaps the time has come to ask a different question: Can we figure out a meaningful conceptualization of intelligence (human or artificial) without common sense?

4.5 So What?

It is common sense to use common sense. It is not common sense to understand common sense – and this may well be enough in itself to show how far AI can go: It cannot learn common sense, yet all knowledge seems to rely on common sense. Here are a few common-sense facts about learning:

---

[17] This is what I call the third level of mastery: novice, advanced, expert, master, grandmaster (Dörfler et al., 2009).

[18] CYC project (by Cycorp): www.cyc.com

- Restricting learning to reinforcement learning means considering only a tiny fraction of learning. It is a similar restriction as limiting knowledge to explicit knowledge.
- Unlike machines, we learn more easily what we are gifted in and find it easier to work hard in those areas. If we are inspired, we also learn better (this can mean different things in specific cases, such as deeper, with less effort, faster). Yes, there are studies showing that it makes no difference whether the teacher is inspiring or dull. However, those studies assume that exams truthfully portray learning.
- Learning is not a simple cumulative process. There are also transformational learning moments, similar to the Eureka moments in creativity. We gain a sudden understanding in these moments, a profound insight that rearranges what we know and is likely to change our approach and even values.

I personally believe in the master–apprentice relationship; it is one of the greatest intellectual treasures we have. It is the only way of learning that makes achieving the highest level of mastery – the grandmaster level – possible. This form of learning will hopefully be popular again, perhaps partly precisely because of AI.

5 Creating

Creativity is intelligence having fun.

Anonymous[19]

This section examines the performance delivered by AI in human realms that feature creativity. The possible usefulness of AI in human creative endeavors is also explored, making a case for AI being able to recognize patterns but not to judge the significance of those patterns. While I argue that AI cannot be creative in the same sense we attribute this word to humans, I leave the door open to the possibility of artificial creativity in an alternative (hitherto unknown) conceptualization. Perhaps somewhat surprisingly, I find that AI can help human creativity in an unexpected way: It can help us "think outside the box."

5.1 AI Performance

In his already mentioned talk at the New Scientist Live event in 2017 (subsection 4.2), the second assertion that Hassabis made was that Google DeepMind's AlphaGo program demonstrated creativity and intuition when it defeated 18-time world champion Lee Sedol in a five-game match of Go. Performance in areas in which humans perform using their creativity may be particularly fruitful to explore in figuring out what we expect from AI – now and in the future. But to get there, let me look into the distant past again for some early clues. The history of AI could be described as a comedy of overstatements. One of the first ones was when in 1957 Simon predicted:

1. That within ten years a digital computer will be the world's chess champion, unless the rules bar it from competition.
2. That within ten years a digital computer will discover and prove an important new mathematical theorem.
3. That within ten years a digital computer will write music that will be accepted by critics as possessing considerable aesthetic value.
4. That within ten years most theories in psychology will take the form of computer programs, or of qualitative statements about the characteristics of computer programs.

(Simon & Newell, 1958: 7–8)

Not a single one of these predictions was met in the suggested timeframe and only the first one in four decades rather than one. What is remarkable about this is that Simon was an exceptional mind, and he was rarely way off in his assessments or predictions. Looking into further details of the one prediction

---

[19] This quote is usually attributed to Albert Einstein, but there is no evidence that he really said this or anything similar – it does not appear in *The Ultimate Quotable Einstein* (Einstein, 2010).

that was eventually fulfilled, and similar extraordinary performances, may help us better understand why these predictions were unsuccessful and what we can expect in the future.

It was in 1997, 40 years after Simon's prediction, that Deep Blue, a computer designed specifically for this purpose, defeated Garry Kasparov, who is possibly the best (human) chess player of all time. The legitimacy of the win could be appealed on the grounds that Deep Blue was adapted between the games, thereby making it impossible to play against a specific style. However, we can accept the win. The second similar performance was the one referenced at the beginning of this section, when in 2016 AlphaGo defeated Go world champion Lee Sedol, and later on numerous other Go grandmasters. While Deep Blue was programmed to play chess, AlphaGo learned to play Go on the basis of about 100,000 learning examples (games downloaded from the Internet) and a few hundred billion games played against itself. Thus AlphaGo obtained a huge database of moves and could replicate the statistical frequency of particular moves leading to win or loss in a particular situation. AlphaGo defeating the best Go players is a fantastic achievement, but it is not the brilliance of the machine; it is the brilliance of its makers. AlphaGo was neither intuitive nor creative. The creators of AlphaGo were both. AlphaGo, in turn, simply looked up the statistical frequency of moves based on hundreds of billions of games and made a move unconstrained by the conventions that humans adopt in playing Go: calculation rather than intuition, and probability rather than creativity.

Let me now look at the specific spectacular performances (see Bory, 2019 for a more detailed discussion). In both cases there was a masterstroke that shocked the human players and was highly praised by the chess and Go grandmasters respectively. In the first case, one of Deep Blue's designers, later on, said that there was a glitch in the system, caused by a bug, which did not allow Deep Blue to select one of the evaluated steps, so it chose a random step instead (Finley, 2012). As in the Chinese Room Argument, it was Kasparov who created the meaning of this step – assigning it long-term strategic considerations. AlphaGo made a move against Sedol that corresponded to all the rules but had never been made by a human Go master. To limit the enormous number of possibilities in Go, the tradition evolved towards playing line 3 or 4 in particular situations, and nobody ever played line 5. However, AlphaGo, during its "training period," played some 300 billion games (which would be many grandmaster lifetimes) against itself and built a database of moves, and the surprising move had a higher probability for a win in that particular situation. The first look at both of these stories suggests that there was no creativity, in the human sense, demonstrated by AI in either case.

What I have laid out so far, I think, makes a sufficiently convincing argument that AI does not think or learn or create the way humans do. However, this does not necessarily mean that AI does not think or learn or create in ways that are different or only partially overlapping with the human ways. To deliver a particular performance, it is not necessary to do it as humans do – and we can see that AI can beat us in areas like the game of Go. All the success stories, however, are in relatively narrow domains. With rare exceptions, this means one single problem area. The rare exceptions include DeepMind, which plays various Atari (an early PC of the 1980s) computer games, and AlphaZero,[20] which plays Go, chess, and shogi. Although covering multiple domains in a single system is a significant step forward, playing several different games is very far from covering a full spectrum of human problem-solving, such as leading an organization, writing a poem, nursing a patient, or enjoying a football game (as a fan). In short, there is convincing evidence that artificially reproducing thinking and learning, and consequently creativity, in a human mode is impossible, at least for the time being. The next subsection looks at conceptualizations of creativity in relation to the performance of AI in order to explore whether AI can be creative in some other sense.

5.2 New and Useful Ideas

There are many claims about how AI will eventually create at the finest level of human creative performance. For instance, Minsky in 1982 suggested that AI will write Shakespeare-level prose within 100 and possibly 50 years (Amabile, 2020). Some believe that creativity of AI is not the future but has already happened: "I believe that in our time computers will be able to perform any cognitive task that a person can perform. I believe that computers already can read, think, learn, create … " (Simon, 1977: 6).

For knowledge and learning, I have shown that AI can only deal with a tiny proportion of what these concepts stand for in the case of humans; that is, only explicit knowledge and only reinforcement learning. How about creativity? Traditionally, definitions of creativity indicate the production of novel and useful ideas (e.g. Amabile, 1983b, 1996). There are minor variations of the two attributes; the first one can be original, novel, new, and/or surprising; the second one is useful, valuable, potentially valuable, appropriate, or correct (Amabile, 1983a). So has AI produced anything new and useful? Of course it

---

[20] The successor of AlphaGo is AlphaGo Zero, which learned Go on its own, without the example games, only playing against itself. AlphaGo Zero beats AlphaGo 100 percent of the time, just as AlphaZero, which can learn Go, chess, and shogi on its own, beats AlphaGo Zero. However, AlphaZero can only play one of the games at a time; if it learns chess, it forgets Go (Heaven, 2019: 166).

has. Specifically, the exceptional performance examples above do not qualify, as in the case of Deep Blue it was a random move and the move by AlphaGo was new to the human Go masters, but it was not new for AlphaGo – it must have been made many times if it had high probability (statistical frequency) for a win.

Furthermore, intuitively, I would be hesitant to consider these achievements creative, as it is fairly visible and algorithmic how they were achieved, while creativity involves intuition, which belongs in the tacit dimension: "[T]here is no such thing as a logical method of having ideas, or a logical reconstruction of this process. My view may be expressed by saying that every discovery contains 'an irrational element,' or 'a creative intuition,' in Bergson's sense" (Popper, 1968: 8).

Of course, if the situation was so simple, it would not need to be elaborated upon any further. There is much more to consider. If we go back to the consideration of the two attributes in the definition of creativity, of course, AI has produced both new and useful things. Not only AI, but also faulty experimental equipment, broken machines, and, yes, human mistakes. Just think about the microwave, the Post-It, penicillin, or the X-ray machine[21] – brilliant inventions achieved by accident. We do not label the accidents or the faulty equipment creative. My point is that there is a hidden third requirement in the definition of creativity: It also needs to be an idea. The microwave, the Post-It, penicillin, and the X-ray machine were not ideas; they only became ideas when the person who looked at them figured out how to leave the old ways of thinking and adopt the new and useful thing as a way of thinking instead. In other words, they made the new and useful "thing" into an idea. Anything that we label creative in a human is either an idea first, which is then materialized, or it is a pattern in reality (a "thing"), which is then made into an idea. Again, we are only looking into human creativity for a reference point. Is it possible, perhaps, to have a different sort of creativity for AI?

If we relax the definition of creativity to include "ideas, problem solutions, or other outputs" (Amabile, 2020: 3), it seems to help – this definition removes the hidden third requirement. Was the famous move of AlphaGo new when AlphaGo made it the first time? It might have been, but randomness has perhaps more to do with this than creativity. Deep Blue's move certainly qualifies, although it does not sound right to me – it was an error. Error, like randomness, does not align for me with the idea of creativity.

Does it help if we bring on board the concept of "appropriate judges," who can evaluate whether an AI outcome is creative and to what extent? This has

---

[21] See further fun examples on the BestLife website: https://bestlifeonline.com/accidental-inventions

worked well in the case of human creativity for several decades (Amabile, 1982) and served as the basis of the Consensual Assessment Technique (CAT), one of the most widespread methods for assessing creativity (Baer, 2020). However, I am not convinced. The inadequacy of the Turing test (as demonstrated, for example, by the Chinese Room Argument) suggests that this is not the case. The new proof constructed by the Logic Theorist was judged by Simon and subsequently Russell to be more elegant than the one by Whitehead and Russell – therefore it should qualify. However, while the details of how the LT did this require some technical knowledge, it is easy to see that the process is transparent and fully explicit, even algorithmic – contrary to how we see the human creative process. We should also not forget that both moves produced by Deep Blue and AlphaGo respectively were judged as creative by top experts.

I am not trying to make a case for something to qualify as creative only if it is done by humans. However, I am also trying to avoid labeling something creative that is less than creative. It seems to me that there are two aspects that I cannot let go of when it comes to creativity: It needs to be an idea, and the process must be nonalgorithmic. This does not mean, of course, that in an area where we use creativity, AI cannot deliver better performance by means other than creativity. If so, this can be an advantage that we can harness – I explore some aspects of this possibility in the next subsection.

5.3 Creating with AI

The previous two subsections show a few particularly remarkable examples of AI success. Although I did argue against calling these performances creative, I do believe that they are extraordinary achievements, and these examples do give us an important glimpse into how AI can be immensely useful for human creativity. It is perhaps not surprising that I am arguing for, instead of *replacing* creatives with AI, *supporting* creatives with AI. This may appear to be a philanthropical standpoint, but in fact it is about good management. What we need to achieve is what Kasparov seems to be doing exceptionally well these days: He plays chess with AI support. In comparison with Stockfish and similar contemporary chess machines, Deep Blue seems closer to a pocket calculator, so Kasparov would not stand a chance. However, as I understand it, Kasparov is exceptionally successful in playing against these chess machines with AI support. So AI alone can be bested by a human expert supported by AI. This performance is what we can hope to achieve in a variety of areas of life and business.

The essence of the story is that humans and AI are good at inherently different things. AI is really good at quickly analyzing large amounts of data and identifying patterns in vast sets of facts; things that require precision. That is why Davenport (2018: 44) says that AI is "analytics on steroids" – which became one of my favorite descriptions of AI. Humans are not very good at these things, and even if we managed to do them, they would take far too long. It is curious that nearly all of our education is focused on this small subset of the human mental capacity, which is not even something most of us like or excel at. Of course, it is not that difficult to figure out why, and we can learn from that. The reason is that we are trying to make what we know more objective; I would even go so far as to say that the purpose is to get rid of all that subjectivity – and it seems that AI is better at all that objective stuff.

What AI is not so good at is judging which pattern is, or may potentially be, significant in the situation at hand – but human experts excel at this. For example, if an oncologist and a chemist are working with some chemicals trying to produce an effective cancer treatment, AI may produce an incredible number of combinations of those chemicals, but it cannot judge which resulting chemicals may be of interest, beyond meeting predefined specifications. However, the oncologist and the chemist may figure out, looking at some of the characteristics of the new chemicals produced by AI, that there are some new (explicitly looked-for or unexpected) characteristics that may be useful for curing cancer. Furthermore, they may also notice things they were not looking for; for example, that those characteristics suggest that one of the resulting chemicals may be useful for curing flu. The reason why AI could not notice these is that the solution is in a different realm of expertise than the problem was – the whole knowledge of the two experts was necessary for figuring out the significance of the discovered pattern. Similarly, designers of fashion, furniture, cars, etc. use AI today for coming up with new models. While AI can deliver new models (by rearranging existing patterns), it is the designer who decides which one is beautiful or cool or repulsive. Therefore, AI can provide pre-processing in the sense of identifying and organizing patterns, and by doing so, it can add immense value to the human creative process (see the protein-folding example in the next subsection). So it seems that what humans are good at is all about values and judgments rather than facts and analytics. It is intuition rather than calculation. Judgments, and particularly value judgments, are always personal and therefore both subjective and intentional (as seen in subsection 3.2).

If we go back to the definition of creativity as a new and useful idea, we could say that in the case of a creative person supported by AI, AI may produce the new and useful, while the creative person produces the idea. It can be the way described above, in an "AI-first" mode, and the idea is subsequently recognized. It can work the other way around as well, in an "idea-first" mode, when the creative person comes up with the essence of what will be created, but it will take a lot of further work to have that materialized. The roles are the same in both cases.

There is an additional, perhaps less trivial, value that AI can add to human creativity. High-level human creativity is closely associated with the mastery of the domain (discipline or problem area). Such a high level of mastery takes time to develop, both at the level of the domain and on the level of the individual. This means that the discipline or problem area will develop its knowledge tradition, which the novices acquire as they engage with the domain; it will become their "inherited background" (Wittgenstein, 1969: 94). This helps with the communication within the domain and the development of a community through common practices, etc., but it is also responsible for thinking "inside the box," imposing unnecessary but conventional limitations. This is why the triumph of AlphaGo revitalized the world of Go; human Go grandmasters started experimenting with new moves, new strategies, and they went beyond the approaches of the traditional schools, etc. Consequently, although it may initially sound surprising, AI can help us think "outside the box" in the best sense of the term.

5.4 Authentic AI

I have noted bombastic future claims and explored extraordinary present achievements, as well as showcasing comparative limitations between AI and the human mind. However, none of these answers the question of what we can expect from AI. When it comes to such projections, we are left with little other than our beliefs. Is it possible that all thinking, learning, creating, feeling, and emoting can be reduced to elementary data manipulations? My answer is no, but it is only my personal belief. Many will answer yes. What should we be doing about AI in either case? I believe that it does not matter too much whether the answer is yes or no to this "ultimate question of AI"; what matters is seeing what AI is capable of and developing it further. We will have to decide the direction of further developments again and again anyway.[22] Of course, a more difficult decision is what we invest into AI development, not only in terms of money but also time, energy, effort, knowledge, and emotions, etc. (cf. Ackermann & Eden, 2011). If AI is the ultimate answer to the problems of poverty, climate change, sustainability, pandemics, natural disasters, world peace, and so forth, by all means, we should be "all in." This is not, however, what I see. I am writing these sentences 10 months into the Covid-19 pandemic, shortly after the

---

[22] This is what I call the principle of *research indirection*, after Robert Chia's principle of *strategic indirection* (Dörfler et al., 2018: 7).

announced vaccine and with rumors floating around about a new strain of the virus. There does not, as yet, appear to be any AI contribution to resolving the pandemic. AI itself cannot be blamed for this; rather, it falls on those who overstate and misrepresent what AI is about. We failed to produce good quality data to provide AI with something to work with. It is a human shortcoming, not an AI shortcoming. A more complete answer to this question will have to wait until we explore the moral issues of AI in the next section; however, raising the question here is useful for addressing the topic of this subsection: the problem of authentic AI.

In order to figure out the problem of authentic AI, it is pertinent to revisit what humans are good at vs. what AI is good at, using the very recent example of AlphaFold (Heaven, 2020). AlphaFold is a DeepMind implementation that forecasts a protein structure based on the sequence of amino acids it is made of, and the structure determines the characteristics of the protein. The result is incredible; AlphaFold's predictions were within an atom's size for dozens of proteins. This has been achieved by building on 50 years of protein research by hundreds of scientists, by DeepMind's team of experts in biology, physics, and computer science, and by using around 170,000 proteins to train the ANN. In several ways, this undertaking resembles Feigenbaum's DENDRAL project (see subsection 2.2). We can see from this story that there is a task division between humans and AI; AlphaFold does the number crunching while the researchers do the experiments and provide the amino acid sequences that they expect to be of interest. It is also useful to see that the group of experts figured out the variables to look at based on the previous 50 years of research.

If the examination of the proteins in the previous examples were to be done by hands-on calculations and experiments, it would take hundreds of times longer to get the results that AlphaFold can produce. However, this does not mean that you could simply tell DeepMind "Go figure out protein structures." Although researchers could use their creativity to figure out how to get the structures without AI, it does not mean that AlphaFold does anything creative. As it seems, figuring out the structures can be done by brute force calculations if the system is set up. Remarkably, at DeepMind the expert group did not use brute force calculations; they used smart calculations, doing the creative work upfront, preparing the material for AlphaFold. We can learn from this that if we do something by creativity, it may or may not be necessary to do it that way; it may be possible to do it by brute force calculations as well. Are all the things that humans do by creativity doable by brute force calculations? I do not think so, and if I am right, then it is very important to figure out what can and what cannot be translated from creativity to calculation force.

This brings us to another creativity problem in relation to AI, which now we are ready for. I have, so far, conveniently skipped the whole area of the arts and creative industries in AI. Reading text produced by AI, having seen AI recipes and having discussed them with Marc Stierand,[23] there was no indication of creativity. I do not have sufficient expertise to judge music and paintings, but my understanding from experts is that AI performance is judged better in these areas. Margaret Boden (2009: 244–245) reports about a program written in the 1980s by the composer David Cope, "which could produce very convincing pastiches of a wide range of famous composers," and about an architectural design program that produced previously unseen houses in the style of Frank Lloyd Wright. Having created a distinction between combinatorial, exploratory, and transformational creativity and having examined in detail how many art-making programs work (Boden, 1998), Boden observes that judging rather than producing something new and useful seems to be where AI falls short – which comes very close to my point, although argued from a very different position.

With these explorations in mind, let me get back to the Turing test for a moment. In subsection 2.4 I noted that the Turing test has been based on the "imitation game," and I do believe that this is the root cause of the failure to produce authentic AI. We talk about AI doing, creating, and solving problems and about human–AI collaboration. We are personifying AI. AI runs (as a program), but it does not create. The program produces, but it does not solve problems. However, those humans who create and solve problems may use AI. There is no human–AI collaboration, as collaboration entails intentionality on both sides; AI is something we made, like a car or a screwdriver, and we use it just like we use those other products and tools. I am not saying this because I am against AI; I am saying this because I am for AI. We need to understand that we must stop the imitation game, and we must stop judging AI based on how well it performs in faking humans. Authentic AI is not like a human. Authentic AI is like AI. Only if we get this right can we maximize the potential of AI, which is incredible.

5.5 So What?

There is a Garfield caricature that I love very much. After being offered a "tuna-like" meal, Garfield quips at Jon: "You know what else is tuna flavored? TUNA!" This is how I feel about authentic AI. Looking at AI this way, here are a few facts:

---

[23] My former PhD student and long-term collaborator, a former chef in Michelin-starred restaurants, an haute cuisine scholar, and the director of the EHL Institute of Business Creativity.

- We do not have anything today that even resembles proof of machine creativity in the human sense of the word. What we have evidence for is astonishing AI performance, which praises those who constructed the machines. The rest is claims, along the lines of "It has played chess and Go well, so next it will write poetry."
- At the World Science Festival (WSF) in New York in 2019, Yann LeCun said that the most challenging thing is to define the goal function right for the AI. The problem is not that the AI cannot follow what you tell it, but rather that it precisely follows what you tell it; however, this is often not what you assume, and we often make assumptions without even realizing it. This description fits most AI failures.
- While there is no evidence of AI creativity, there is ample evidence that AI can identify and/or produce patterns that are useful for creative people. What AI cannot do is judge the significance or value of the found or generated patterns. That is why we should focus on enabling people to create with AI support better than without it.

In my view, the achievement of creativity has to be an idea. Regardless of how new and useful something is, it cannot stem from creativity if it is not an idea. However, not everyone and everything needs to be creative; many tasks do not involve ideas, value judgments, intuition, or social and emotional considerations. In these areas, AI may outperform us sooner or later.

6 Moral Issues

All animals are equal, but some animals are more equal than others.[24]

George Orwell

Starting in fall 2017, I delivered 20 talks over the course of about two and a half years on AI and the human mind. Many of the occasions were conferences, at which AI scholars as well as AI vendors gave talks, followed by their audiences asking questions. Every single time, the pattern was the same: Scholars were talking about their research, vendors about the features of their products, and the audience was, without exception, asking about ethics. Will our data be used in an ethical manner? Will we be safe? Is there anything to prevent AI from harming us? Will AI take my job? Does AI make diversity problems worse? In other words, "Okay, so this is what your AI can do, but can we trust it?"

6.1 Trust in AI?

At those conferences, as well as in various committees and laboratories, I often ended up discussing "trust in AI" with experts (usually both academics and practitioners). On many occasions, the problem was posited as "how do we increase trust in AI?" This is the wrong question, as I told them many times. Trust must be earned. What you need to do is to build *trustworthy AI*. To be fair, most of these people genuinely wanted to do the right thing. If, however, someone raised the question of, for instance, a self-driving car killing its passenger or the children playing ball on the street, their response was along the lines of "you tell us, and we program it that way." They could not usually even grasp that people were not asking about which outcome it would be. People are uncomfortable about a machine handling such situations; they want to decide whether they die or not. This example also brings the notion of responsibility into the discussion: People do not want to hand over such responsibility to machines – responsibility is also a concept that CEOs find it easy to relate to. The people asking the questions typically did not know much about AI, the human mind, or ethics. The people who tried to answer the questions, with rare exceptions, had a lot of technical knowledge about AI, but they did not know more about the human mind or ethics than those who were asking. This led to a series of futile conversations. You need a philosopher to facilitate the thinking about the ethical questions of AI. I try to unpack

---

[24] A proclamation by the pigs who control the government in the novel *Animal Farm*, by George Orwell.

the problem here, starting with trust and slipping over into more generic moral issues surrounding AI.

Among humans, there are two kinds of trust: trusting the competence and trusting the person. We could expect that the first kind is transferable to machines. We usually trust our laptops to save the documents we are working on and, with very, very rare exceptions, this is justified. When it does not work, we swear at the "stupid machine" and look for the most recent backup. In general, we have figured this out; however, many are aware of the misalignment between the stories and promises of AI on the one hand and the experience of what it delivers on the other hand. The "mistakes" are in every single case some kind of easy fix, but why were they not fixed in advance, then? There is a recent example about the Covid-19 vaccine distribution algorithm from Stanford that left out frontline doctors (Guo & Hao, 2020). It is an easy fix, for sure – however, if such a banal mistake could occur, how can we trust smart technology? Furthermore, transparency, which typically applies to analytical tools, does not apply anymore – we cannot follow step by step what AI does. What we can do is not trust it and check what it delivers against common sense. But is that good enough?

The second type of trust is about trusting that the person will (try to) do the right thing. However, what the right thing is depends on our moral positioning; on our value system. The idea of trusting the person is very much the approach of *virtue ethics*, according to which we trust people we regard as virtuous. If we are proponents of *consequentialist ethics*, we are only looking at the outcome. The subscribers of *deontology* (also referred to as rule-based ethics) believe that it is the action, and therefore the intentions that lead to the action, rather than the consequences that we need to observe, as the outcomes depend on many other things besides what we do. As it is usually too late once we see the consequences, it seems appealing to look for intentions. This is problematic again, however, in the case of AI, as AI does not have intentions. It cannot, as intentions are also rooted in the tacit dimension: "I have now expanded the function of understanding into that of knowing what we intend, what we mean, or what we do. To this we may add now that nothing that is said, written or printed, can ever mean anything in itself: for it is only a person who utters something – or who listens to it or reads it – who can mean something by it" (Polányi, 1959: 22).

We could, perhaps, expect AI to get a representation of our value systems by learning from our decisions. However, acquiring the values from a database of decisions made by different people has two significant limitations: (1) only what is in the database can be taken into consideration, and there may be and will be other variables that are not recorded, and (2) there may be values that we do not want to replicate (see, for example, Hao, 2020 on a predictive policing system that perpetuates corrupt practices). Furthermore, this approach very much resembles the CYC project on modeling common sense (subsection 4.4), which consumed enormous effort without any success whatsoever.

Furthermore, it looks like we cannot acquire a value system from more than one person, as people have their own individual moral compasses, meaning that each person's value system is unique. Whom do we choose, then, as the ultimate decision taker; whose value judgments will loom over everyone's fate? If we did find such a person whose moral judgment we would all be happy to accept, we would then need a few hundred thousand decisions if these were as simple as a protein structure, and perhaps a few hundred billion if it were more like a game of Go. There is bad news in this respect as well: Moral decisions are far more complex and versatile and cover greater scope than a game of Go. So we cannot have a sufficient number of examples to train the ANN.

AI scholars and vendors often assert that there is a great advantage for AI in the area of values: AI is not biased, it applies the value system consistently without exception, it does not get tired, it cannot be in a bad mood, etc. This is, however, an exceptionally good example of misrepresentation. In fact, bias only makes sense if we know the correct answer, and then the bias is a deviation from this. If something is so simple that we can know the generic right answer, we do not even need AI, only process automation; there is no decision to be made. There are no moral issues to consider. These come up when it is unclear what is right, when we are trying to choose the lesser of two evils, when alternatives have some good and some bad characteristics, and so forth. In other words, in situations that we face many times a day and which we have somehow learned how to find our way around.

6.2 Mistakes and Consequences

Think of a brilliantly designed robot surgeon: It has vastly increased precision compared to a human hand; it can visually register thousands of times finer details than humans can see; when stitching a wound, it is always perfectly even. Of course, it can only do simple operations, as during an operation there are too many things to see and to make sense of, often things that were not expected to be seen in relation to things that are not seen at all, etc. So it can only do the simple operations but not the really difficult ones – the top surgeons are proud, as they are still needed to do the most difficult operations. However, the next generation of surgeons is growing up. They never get any level of practice, as the simple operations are done by the robot surgeon. Should the new human surgeons start their practice doing brain surgery? Of course not; nobody suggests that – however, this is exactly what can happen. In the "Air France 447 Disaster" (Oliver et al., 2017a, 2017b), the autopilot handed over the control to the pilots due to unusual conditions, something that an average pilot, arguably, should have been able to handle; however, the pilots, constantly relying on the autopilot, were not up to the task. All 228 passengers and crew died. My description is, naturally, oversimplified but not incorrect in principle, and it is easy to see how similar issues can emerge in many areas, even if the consequences are, at least apparently, less severe.

It would be prudent to caution against arguments that cite, for example, statistical data on road accidents caused by human error to support claims regarding the safety of self-driving cars. These arguments are supposed to dismiss the fears of AI failure, suggesting that there will be still fewer accidents than if humans were driving. The problem is that there is only statistical evidence for the accidents that happened due to human error. There is no statistical evidence regarding how many accidents have been avoided thanks to human skills, decisions, etc., as the accidents did not happen. We also should not forget that if AI is put on the streets, it will have to drive within the messy behavior of human drivers; the whole transportation system will not be replaced overnight by exclusively self-driving vehicles.

We tend to think of all that precision – for example, of visual input – as a good thing. However, Heaven (2019: 164) lists numerous examples of "fooling the AI." Remarkably, random replacement of a single (or very few) pixel(s) may succeed in this; something we would never even notice with the naked eye. It is not a problem that AI makes mistakes every now and then; humans do as well. The problem is that we have no idea how a previously recognized lion is identified by the same software as a library, having had a few pixels changed, when it looks the same to us. On the one hand, we cannot predict these mistakes, and they may be extremely serious. A striking example was when, luckily in a test, a medical chatbot by Nabla, using OpenAI's GPT-3, recommended suicide to a fake patient (Daws, 2020). On the other hand, skilled hackers may use these to attack AI, causing malfunctions and perhaps even completely reprograming it if they can figure out what a particular set of pixel changes may lead to. I do not know of any real examples, but we could easily end up in a "war games" scenario; just imagine if you could set up a hackathon and tell some talented hackers that it was a computer game, something simulated . . .

However, what is most alarming here is misattribution; Heaven quotes Jürgen Schmidhuber, an AI researcher from the Dalle Molle Institute for Artificial Intelligence Research, as stating: "Pattern recognition is extremely powerful, he says – good enough to have made companies such as Alibaba, Tencent,

Amazon, Facebook and Google the most valuable in the world" (Heaven, 2019: 165).

No, pattern recognition did not make these companies so incredibly valuable – brilliant ideas did. Many brilliant ideas. Extraordinary leadership. I would even say that at least some of these companies are valuable in spite of extremely bad pattern recognition, typical of what I like to call "stupid smart devices." For example, having purchased the children's paperback edition of *Harry Potter and the Philosopher's Stone*, Amazon kept recommending to me the other three variants of the same volume – it did not recognize that these are not similar books but the same book with different covers. A friend traveled to Peru when he was 62, for the first time in his life, and for the next 5 years he received daily offers for flights to Lima. He likes to travel, and, like many passionate travelers, he likes visiting new places. This is a major travel pattern, probably typical of many people, yet travel suggestions typically work against it.

These examples are all about easy-to-grasp mistakes (so why they have not been fixed for years?); however, there is something else common among them: They are all about values, which means that they are directly relevant to moral issues. In many ways, values are similar to common sense (subsection 4.4) in as much as we often cannot account for their origins; they form highly complex patterns and seem impossible to capture by AI. Furthermore, we do not only learn the values that we observe, choosing among contradictory ones from our teachers, parents, etc. We also create values. "I shall show, for example, that when originality breeds new values, it breeds them tacitly, by implication; we cannot choose explicitly a set of new values, but must submit to them by the very act of creating or adopting them" (Polányi, 1966b: xix).

Most often, we cannot put a finger on when a particular value has been created. Often, we just recognize that they are already there; that we have been following them for some time already. Or someone else recognizes this for us. Our values also form complex systems that, like our concepts (subsection 3.4), may feature "strange loops" (Hofstadter, 1979). The messy, complex system of values, however, comes together in a moral compass pointing to right or wrong every time we face a moral dilemma or any dilemma that has a moral aspect. In contrast, AI does not "have a good model of how to pick out what matters" (Heaven, 2019: 164). Such judgments of "what matters" are at the core of what AI cannot do. This is where common sense and wisdom are very similar. Weizenbaum, who built ELIZA (the first AI to pass the Turing test: see subsections 2.4 and 3.4), wrote the first book that explicitly raised the issue of morality in AI (Weizenbaum, 1976). Instead of focusing on what AI research can or cannot achieve, he argued that there are areas where AI should not be used, regardless of what it is capable of. His argument was built on moral rather than technical grounds, and his main point was that there is no space for AI in areas of moral judgment, as that requires wisdom and empathy.

6.3 Ethics and Law

There is a tricky relationship between moral and normative regulation. Moral (or fine) regulation is about what is the right thing to do according to a particular morality, and the consequence of a moral error is that we feel bad about it. In contrast, normative regulations, such as various levels of legal regulations, organizational standards and procedures, etc., prescribe legitimate ways of doing things and assign penalties for deviating from these. Ethics and law are the disciplines that study the moral and the legal systems respectively. Of course, most legal regulations are rooted in moral regulations, but once they are codified, they are not a matter of morality any longer; for example, it does not matter if it is morally right or wrong to kill, as it is against the law. It is even possible for the moral and the legal views to be in conflict. For instance, stealing a loaf of bread to feed your hungry child as a last resort may be illegal and morally right at the same time. What I want to illustrate with these few points on moral and legal regulations is that while legal regulations could be handled by AI similarly to "legal" protein structures (see the AlphaFold example in subsection 5.4), moral regulations cannot.

Naturally, if the legal regulation was as simple as it may seem from my previous description, we would only need AI, and we would not need incredibly expensive lawyers. Why are lawyers, particularly good lawyers, so expensive? Because they can read between the lines, because they can offer meaningful interpretations, and, yes, because they can play the system. To put it differently, the legal system is incomplete, and it is being supplemented by moral regulation. In the legal profession, the use of AI is particularly exciting, as there is a reasonably clear distinction between where the codification (or precedence) ends and where the interpretation begins. In other words, along the dimensions of knowing, learning, and creating, it is clear where AI can do the job and what needs a human mind. This is probably the reason that the master–apprentice relationship has survived longer in legal firms than in almost any other kind of organization (including academia). The significance of the interpretation in law, and therefore of morality, cannot be overstated. In case law, a new case is judged on the basis of previous cases. However, the tricky question is which previous cases are relevant and how to find them – AI can be incredibly useful in finding potentially similar cases, but it takes human judgment to decide which precedence cases to use. It is similar, although arguably less trivial, in codified law, where the rules are usually clear but their scope leaves space for interpretation and judgment.

In addition to the previously noted reasons, there is also a statistical reason for this: The "sample" often does not represent the "population." This may cause a generic problem of disregarding the extraordinary (Dörfler & Stierand, 2019), which can be frustrating if you are looking to hire the extraordinary. However, in terms of ethics and law, for AI, a genius can be as much a deviation from the norm as a criminal.

The same logic will also cause issues in crime profiling; we can find out about the false positives (indicted as criminals but found innocent) but not about the false negatives (criminals not identified). Of course, it would be nonsense not to use such an incredible and powerful tool as AI to support law enforcement – as long as we support the police officers rather than substitute them with AI. Predictive policing as an automated process can be a disaster (Hao, 2020), but as an early warning system, helping to select what experts should make judgments about can be helpful. Again, it is about the interpretation.

There is a part of all legal systems that emphasizes this significance of the interpretation; it is the jury system. The jury is not supposed to be objective but inter-subjective. In other words, the interpretation is up to those 12 or so people; they do not only interpret things for themselves but also together, arguing with each other, trying out the various narratives, thinking together. The same approach also works reasonably well in science; Popper suggested that inter-subjectivity is the second best thing in the absence of objectivity (Popper, 1968: 22). I have been trying to show so far where and how we will face problems when trying to delineate the roles of AI and humans in the presence of moral dilemmas and how this fits within the legal system. I have not, however, provided any answers regarding what to do about these problems, as they are far too diverse; all we can know is that we need to pay exceptional attention to them, as the consequences can be extremely serious as well as far-reaching. Half-grounded arguments will not do. Using AI, technically, self-reinforcing and pre-emptive legal regulation can become possible. However, this would be detrimental to individual liberties and bring the whole democratic system into question. If we proceeded that way, AI would become the dream of all dictators.

Another area of legal and moral problems surrounding AI is whether we should protect AI from humans. While this may sound inconceivable at this time, Kate Darling (2019) from MIT argues that we should protect AI-based products, such as robots, chatbots, and digital assistants. Not because the machines need this, but because we humans do. Going a step further, Wiklund (2020) suggests that "[t]o the extent that AI is able to experience enjoyment and suffering, it is reasonable that we have the same moral obligations towards AI as we do towards animals."

(See a few more possible approaches discussed in Coeckelbergh, 2020.) Today, machines can be bullied, of course without consequences for the machines. However, this may lead to the development of bullying behavior, and those who would torture robots and behave abusively to chatbots may be on the way to becoming abusive to humans. An alternative argument is that if the bully can abuse the machines, perhaps machines purposefully built to this end would satisfy this need, and the bully would be less abusive to other people. We do not really know which argument is correct, as usual; probably there can be a little bit of both. I tend to side with Darling; just like protecting dogs from being abused is more important to people than to dogs, it also sounds sensible to protect AI. However, it is certainly a problem worth thinking about. Let me take this problem to an extreme: Maybe you have heard of sex robots. Today they can be abused with no limitation, as they are mere machines. However, there is evidence, all the way back to Aristotle, that habituation normalizes negative behavior.

6.4 The Singularity

I think that I have managed to depict convincingly that the moral issues are some of the hardest problems that we are currently facing in the area of AI, and we will have several decades to try to cope with them. All the other problems that we need to figure out regarding knowing and learning and creating are also incorporated into the moral issues, and there is much more. Furthermore, we are at a stage when each moral AI dilemma is unique; there are no generic answers. It is important to ask better questions and provide some thinking tools for finding personalized answers for the unique problems. We are likely to learn the most about AI over the next few decades by exploring moral issues rather than from advances in technology (which does not mean that we should stop advancing technology).

The ultimate moral issue is the so-called singularity,[25] possibly leading to the doomsday scenario of AI. Where are we with this? Is the singularity as near as Ray Kurzweil (2005) argues? I do not think so. The crucial point in this variant is the concept of consciousness. There are some who promise that we will be able to download consciousness into a computer within five years (and this was already being said five years ago). How far we are from this? Well, technologically probably not that far, in as much as we can already connect a microchip to the human nervous system. The problem is on the other side: We still have almost no idea what consciousness is. We do know that our phenomenal experiences have

---

[25] Singularity is a point of no return. It signifies a special set of conditions in which or beyond which the behavior of the system cannot be predicted and/or described. With reference to AI, it is usually considered as the point at which the super-smart computer awakens to consciousness.

something to do with it, which David Chalmers (1998) calls the hard problem of consciousness. What is it we want to download? Where is it?

The problem that is at the core of my argument can be observed in many areas of AI. Newell and Simon (subsection 2.1) make a leap from playing chess and proving mathematical theorems to understanding English prose. Elon Musk[26] offers a convincing argument (and demonstration) of how Neuralink can, for example, help disabled people regain the ability to walk or hear or see, as the chip can bypass/replace damaged neural pathways. However, this does not justify or explain how we would store our memories on those same chips – and if we did, we still cannot get from memories to consciousness. The AI pioneer Terry Winograd (1990) traces the problem back to Thomas Hobbes (1651), who described thinking (reason) as computation of symbols. It is as if a geologist were studying rocks and expected that acquiring more data (and perhaps knowledge) about rocks would lead to a deep understanding of the nature of trees and frogs and human societies. Many in the AI world expect that AI can be smarter than humans, as it is faster doing those things that it can do. However, this is only a small part of what humans can do, and connecting more neurons or processing more data of the same kind or further increasing the speed would not necessarily, or is even likely to, lead to the emergence of thought, let alone consciousness.

Musk (2018) has a slightly different take on the singularity problem. He comments on AI and specifically on DeepMind, as it is an AI that has access to all the Google servers, and everything is on those servers. The purpose of DeepMind here is to optimize the energy consumption of the servers, but, as Musk argues, a small update can make it access all the data on those servers, all of *our* data, and do with it what it pleases. Do we need to be worried about this? Technically, access to data should not be particularly difficult for a hacker who can break into Google's servers. Musk also talks about his variant of the doomsday scenario; in his vision, AI is not going to hate us, but we might just happen to be in the way of achieving its goal and so it destroys us – the same as we do not hate ants, but if they are in our way, we destroy them. I would like to note here that we (humans) have not killed all ants. And yes, we have made quite a few species extinct, but as we are getting smarter about this, we are doing more to protect them. So if those who speak of superintelligence are right, maybe we have nothing to fear; maybe the super-smart computer will also have a superior moral standing. In either case, according to Spender, we do not need to worry about the singularity:

---

[26] https://youtu.be/UdWdhPp-1yE

If a singularity really is coming, it's beyond our ability to understand it. Machines might become conscious – they may be already – but the odds are, we won't be able to recognize it. If the singularity is not coming, then it's just empty dogmatism. Hence our task is always more practical – to bring a machine's functionality, as we comprehend it, to bear on our world and our projects, answering "What does it mean to us?" rather than puzzling about what we might mean to them. (Spender, 2015)

This leads me to my doomsday scenario. As I do not believe in a thinking machine in the human sense of thinking and feeling and emotions and consciousness, I am not afraid that the machine that awakens to consciousness will turn against us. However, there is a realistic chance that we (humans) will assign a task to the not-so-smart AI that, because of a machine mistake (see the picture recognition problems in subsection 6.2), leads to a disaster. It is not the AI's error that makes this possible but the human error, over-enthusiastically telling AI to do what it is not supposed to.

On a smaller scale, this is the ultimate level of what needs to be carefully considered in each AI implementation. We need to be meticulous about what tasks we assign to AI; the responsibility for AI lies with those who decide about AI implementations – the CEOs.

6.5 So What?

While ethics and morality may sound too philosophical, responsibility and duty are concepts that all CEOs work with daily. If the machine thinks, it should be held responsible for its actions; its makers are off the hook. Here are a few comments on facts in the area of trust, ethics, and responsibility:

- For those who do not understand AI, the term "thinking machine" sounds scary and not trustworthy. However, we should clarify that we can comprehend AI, even if it is not fully transparent in what it does step by step. What we do not understand so well is the human mind.
- Not many people want to hear that we need to learn some statistics in order to become better at discerning fact from fiction and judging the robustness of statements. It is essential to understand the claims and not to simply shut down as soon as someone mentions percentages. A student complained once about my marking, noting that about half of the class performed below average. In fact, it was the definition of average with which he disagreed . . .
- One of the most detrimental things to trust in AI is that AI sometimes makes elementary mistakes, like mistaking a picture of a lion for a library due to the change of a few pixels. The scary thing about this is that it seems

inconceivable how such a mistake could happen. How can we trust something that makes such elementary mistakes to operate a self-driving car?

When I interviewed several Nobel Laureates, it became clear that they were exceptionally good at switching between the "big picture" and the detail (cf. McGilchrist, 2019), which I call "seeing the essence." While it sounds like we could program the values we want (detail), applying those values in particular situations (the big picture) seems to be exceptionally complex – something particularly human.

7 Final Commentary

No mind is thoroughly well organized that is deficient in a sense of humor.
Samuel Taylor Coleridge

This short book concludes with a final commentary instead of a conclusion, emphasizing that the story is nowhere near the end, and we will need to come back from time to time and revise it. My goal has been to offer some suggestions regarding a useful perspective on AI which can help us create a better narrative for our human future. Although many details have been omitted, I believe I managed to depict a big picture with a thick brush and broad brushstrokes; that is, this picture is high-level, comprehensive, and although it does not include all the details, it can be helpful for making sense of any details, existing ones as well as new ones to come. I hope that offering my view on AI in this book, as a sensible AI enthusiast, describing the limitations and strengths of AI, I can help CEOs make sense of AI, delineating facts from beliefs, in order to make the best use of AI for their organizations.

A quarter of a century ago, the management guru Peter Drucker stated:

> Ever since the new data processing tools first emerged 30 or 40 years ago, businesspeople have both overrated and underrated the importance of information in the organization. We – and I include myself – overrated the possibilities to the point where we talked of computer-generated "business models" that could make decisions and might even be able to run much of the business. But we also grossly underrated the new tools; we saw in them the means to do better what executives were already doing to manage their organizations. (Drucker, 1995: 54)

We are in a bit of a similar position, I believe, regarding AI today; we are both underestimating and overestimating what AI can bring us. Both mistakes lead to less good use of AI than is possible. Furthermore, there is too much emphasis on the short term. As Heaven (2019: 165) argues, quoting Gary Marcus of the New York University, "[d]eep learning is so useful in the short term that people have lost sight of the long term" – yet he believes that hybrid systems are the long-term way forward. I also believe that synthesizing what has been achieved and learned about AI in various parts of the fragmented field can bring substantial further gains. Furthermore, although it is generally accepted that ethics is the hottest topic in AI, I believe that this is also the area in which the greatest learning about AI will occur over the next decade or so. We have a very large number of moral issue cases, with new ones coming in on a daily basis, and we have to treat them with exceptional care as individual cases. As we are obtaining the individual answers, a deeper learning will take place that may not lead us to generic answers but that will help us become better and faster at developing unique answers. Just like a psychoanalyst or an executive coach, who does not do the same thing for every client but learns from each case and becomes a better and better psychoanalyst or coach.

Although this book does not make huge demands on the reader on the technological side, it is heavy on psychology and philosophy. I believe that this is unavoidable; the CEO needs to become a moral philosopher and a philosopher of the mind. Just as Ann Cunliffe (2009) argued, the CEO needs to become a "philosopher leader."

As argued and showcased throughout the book, AI is still about data, even if about an exceptionally sophisticated processing of data. It is about finding patterns and combinations of patterns. However, it is the human mind that can make sense of those patterns, that can judge their (possible) significance. While AI can help a lot in data-rich areas of explicit knowledge and reinforcement learning, it cannot deal with tacit knowledge, nor with emotions, feelings, and beliefs that affect knowledge and learning, or other forms of learning, including inspiration, talent, and master–apprentice relationships. AI can generate new patterns, particularly from a combination of previous patterns, but cannot judge which one is good or beautiful or cool or sexy. As Davenport (2018) says, AI does not make better decisions, but rather it can make our decisions better informed.

Based on the above, to me it is clear that AI does not make strategy, but it is a strategic decision *whether*, for *what*, and *how* we use AI – and this is why every CEO needs to know a little bit about AI. With reference to the realms of *known*, *unknown*, and *unknowable* (subsection 1.2), for the known, we do not need AI; we only need well-thought-through databases and data transactions. In the unknown, AI can be extremely useful, finding patterns in the data and filtering data as well as patterns, but it will still be the subject experts who will need to make sense of these. In the realm of the unknowable, we will need to rely primarily on our intuition, but AI can still be useful; it can scan the nearby data environment and present us with patterns, which we can judge. It can also scan the long-range data horizon for possibly useful patterns. It is mostly complementary to the CEO's intuition; the CEO does not look for predetermined signs, but the CEO observes and makes sense of the emerging signs. AI can complement this by adding to what emerges on the CEO's radar.

In the words of Coleridge above, beware of any conceptualization of intelligence that does not include humor. With a couple of colleagues, we came to the same conclusion the hard way: Exploring the levels of systemic complexity by Boulding (1956), we tried for years to figure out how to make a sound distinction between the animal and the human level. We ended up with the following: *humans can create and understand jokes*. This may sound superficial and funny, but actually, the statement covers an exceptionally complex set of cognitive conditions. First, we must have memory – and it must be historic memory – as well as the capability of abstraction, reasoning, and self-consciousness beyond mere self-awareness, just to mention a few things. If I were to do a Turing test, that would be the first thing I would try.

My final advice is that we should not think of AI as making us smarter. AI amplifies what we've got, so if we happen to be stupid, it will amplify that too. This means that the CEO can probably get the greatest benefits of AI by allocating it to support the top experts rather than to replace the mediocre. As I have been saying for a few years now, the greatest achievements in the future will come from smart people using smart technology.

The Author

As a practitioner, I spearheaded the development of a piece of AI software (knowledge-based expert system shell *Doctus*) from 1999 to 2004, and I have been using it since 1998 as a knowledge engineer to support C-level decision takers as well as knowledge workers by modeling expert knowledge. As a scholar, I am interested in the human mind, particularly phenomena such as intuition, creativity, and the master–apprentice relationship. In order to understand the thinking and learning of "grandmasters" at the highest level of mastery, I have conducted a series of interviews with 20 top scientists, including 17 Nobel Laureates. Bringing these two sides of my work together, over the past three years I have delivered 20+ talks globally, including a TEDx talk, and written two encyclopedia entries on AI (Dörfler, 2020, 2022).

References

Aaronson, S. (2014, June 9). My Conversation with "Eugene Goostman," the Chatbot That's All Over the News for Allegedly Passing the Turing Test. *Shtetle-Optimized*. www.scottaaronson.com/blog/?p=1858

Ackermann, F. & Eden, C. (2011). *Making Strategy: Mapping Out Strategic Success*. London: SAGE Publications. http://books.google.co.uk/books? id=Ln1PQLi-flIC

Amabile, T. M. (1982). Social Psychology of Creativity: A Consensual Assessment Technique. *Journal of Personality and Social Psychology*, **43** (5), 997–1013. https://doi.org/10.1037/0022-3514.43.5.997

Amabile, T. M. (1983a). The Social Psychology of Creativity: A Componential Conceptualization. *Journal of Personality and Social Psychology*, **45**(2), 357–376. https://doi.org/10.1037/0022-3514.45.2.357

Amabile, T. M. (1983b). *The Social Theory of Creativity*. New York: Springer-Verlag.

Amabile, T. M. (1996). *Creativity in Context: Update to the Social Psychology of Creativity*. Boulder, CO: Westview Press.

Amabile, T. M. (2020). GUIDEPOST: Creativity, Artificial Intelligence, and a World of Surprises. *Academy of Management Discoveries*, **6**(3), 351–354. https://doi.org/10.5465/amd.2019.0075

Aron, J. (2011, September 6). Software Tricks People into Thinking It Is Human. *New Scientist*. www.newscientist.com/article/dn20865-software-tricks-people-into-thinking-it-is-human

Baer, J. (2020). The Consensual Assessment Technique. In V. Dörfler & M. Stierand, eds., *Handbook of Research Methods on Creativity*. Cheltenham: Edward Elgar, pp. 166–177. https://doi.org/10.4337 /9781786439659.00020

Baracskai, Z. & Velencei, J. (2002, November 6–7). Important Characteristics for a Knowledge Engineer. 12th Annual Conference of Business Information Technology, Manchester, UK.

Bas, A., Sinclair, M., & Dörfler, V. (2022). Sensing: The Elephant in the Room of Management Learning. *Management Learning*. https://doi.org/10.1177/ 13505076221077226

von Bertalanffy, L. (1981). *A Systems View of Man*. Boulder, CO: Westview Press.

Boden, M. A. (1998). Creativity and Artificial Intelligence. *Artificial Intelligence*, **103**(1), 347–356. https://doi.org/10.1016/S0004-3702(98) 00055-1

Boden, M. A. (2009). Creativity: How Does It Work? In M. Krausz, D. Dutton, & K. Bardsley, eds., *The Idea of Creativity.* Leiden: Brill, pp. 237–250.

Bory, P. (2019). Deep New: The Shifting Narratives of Artificial intelligence from Deep Blue to AlphaGo. *Convergence*, **25**(4), 627–642. https://doi.org/10.1177/1354856519829679

Boulding, K. E. (1956). General Systems Theory: The Skeleton of Science. *Management Science*, **2**(3), 197–208. https://doi.org/10.1287/mnsc.2.3.197

Boulding, K. E. (1966). The Economics of Knowledge and the Knowledge of Economics. *American Economic Review*, **56**(1/2), 1–13. www.jstor.org/stable/1821262

Chalmers, D. J. (1998). *The Conscious Mind: In Search of a Fundamental Theory*, paperback ed. New York: Oxford University Press.

Chomsky, N. (1957/2002). *Syntactic Structures*, 2nd ed. New York: Mouton de Gruyter.

Clarke, A. C. (1962/2013). *Profiles of the Future: An Inquiry into the Limits of the Possible*. London: Gollancz. https://books.google.co.uk/books?id=8_AcAQAAMAAJ

Coeckelbergh, M. (2020). Should We Treat Teddy Bear 2.0 as a Kantian Dog? Four Arguments for the Indirect Moral Standing of Personal Social Robots, with Implications for Thinking About Animals and Humans. *Minds and Machines*, **31**, 337–360. https://doi.org/10.1007/s11023-020-09554-3

Cunliffe, A. L. (2009). The Philosopher Leader: On Relationalism, Ethics and Reflexivity – A Critical Perspective to Teaching Leadership. *Management Learning*, **40**(1), 87–101. https://doi.org/10.1177/1350507608099315

Damasio, A. R. (1995/2005). *Descartes' Error: Emotion, Reason, and the Human Brain*. New York: Avon Books.

Darling, K. (2019, March 27). Why We Should Show Machines Some Respect [Interview]. *Forbes*. www.forbes.com/sites/insights-intelai/2019/03/27/why-we-should-show-machines-some-respect

Davenport, T. H. (2018). *The AI Advantage: How to Put the Artificial Intelligence Revolution to Work*. Cambridge, MA: MIT Press.

Davenport, T. H. & O'Dell, C. (2019, March 18). Explainable AI and the Rebirth of Rules. *Forbes*. www.forbes.com/sites/tomdavenport/2019/03/18/explainable-ai-and-the-rebirth-of-rules

Davenport, T. H. & Prusak, L. (2000). *Working Knowledge: How Organizations Manage What They Know*, paperback ed. Boston, MA: Harvard Business School Press.

Daws, R. (2020, October 28). Medical Chatbot Using OpenAI's GPT-3 Told a Fake Patient to Kill Themselves. *AI News*. https://artificialintelligence-news.com/2020/10/28/medical-chatbot-openai-gpt3-patient-kill-themselves

Dörfler, V. (2010). Learning Capability: The Effect of Existing Knowledge on Learning. *Knowledge Management Research & Practice*, **8**(4), 369–379. https://doi.org/10.1057/kmrp.2010.15

Dörfler, V. (2020). Artificial Intelligence. In M. A. Runco & S. R. Pritzker, eds., *Encyclopedia of Creativity*, 3rd ed., Vol. 1. Oxford: Academic Press, pp. 57–64. https://doi.org/10.1016/B978-0-12-809324-5.23863-7

Dörfler, V. (2021). Looking Back on a Framework for Thinking about Group Decision Support Systems. In D. M. Kilgour & C. Eden, eds., *Handbook of Group Decision and Negotiation*, 2nd ed., Vol. 2. Cham: Springer, pp. 837–860. https://doi.org/10.1007/978-3-030-49629-6_32

Dörfler, V. (2022). Artificial Intelligence. In J. Mattingly, ed., *The SAGE Encyclopedia of Theory in Science, Technology, Engineering, and Mathematics*. Thousand Oaks, CA: SAGE Publications.

Dörfler, V. & Ackermann, F. (2012). Understanding Intuition: The Case for Two Forms of Intuition. *Management Learning*, **43**(5), 545–564. https://doi.org/10.1177/1350507611434686

Dörfler, V., Baracskai, Z., & Velencei, J. (2009, August 7–11). *Knowledge Levels: 3-D Model of the Levels of Expertise*. AoM 2009: 69th Annual Meeting of the Academy of Management, Chicago, IL. The Academy of Management. www.researchgate.net/publication/308339223

Dörfler, V. & Bas, A. (2020a). Intuition: Scientific, Non-Scientific or Unscientific? In M. Sinclair, ed., *Handbook of Intuition Research as Practice*. Cheltenham: Edward Elgar, pp. 293–305. https://doi.org/10.4337/9781788979757.00033

Dörfler, V. & Bas, A. (2020b, August 7–11). *Tools for Exploring the Unknowable: Intuition vs. Artificial Intelligence*. AoM 2020: 80th Annual Meeting of the Academy of Management, Vancouver, BC. The Academy of Management. www.researchgate.net/publication/342135191

Dörfler, V. & Bas, A. (unpublished). Understanding Uncertainty: Known, Unknown, and Unknowable.

Dörfler, V. & Eden, C. (2017, August 4–8). *Becoming a Nobel Laureate: Patterns of a Journey to the Highest Level of Expertise*. AoM 2017: 77th Annual Meeting of the Academy of Management, Atlanta, GA. The Academy of Management. https://doi.org/10.5465/AMBPP.2017.12982 abstract

Dörfler, V. & Eden, C. (2019). Understanding "Expert" Scientists: Implications for Management and Organization Research. *Management Learning*, **50**(5), 534–555, Article 135050761986665. https://doi.org/10.1177/1350507619866652

Dörfler, V. & Stierand, M. (2017). The Underpinnings of Intuition. In J. Liebowitz, J. Paliszkiewicz, & J. Gołuchowski, eds., *Intuition, Trust, and Analytics*. Boca Raton, FL: Taylor & Francis, pp. 3–20. https://doi.org/ 10.1201/9781315195551-1

Dörfler, V. & Stierand, M. (2018, August 10–14). *Understanding Indwelling through Studying Intuitions of Nobel Laureates and Top Chefs*. AoM 2018: 78th Annual Meeting of the Academy of Management, Chicago, IL. The Academy of Management.

Dörfler, V. & Stierand, M. (2019). Extraordinary: Reflections on Sample Representativeness. In I. Lebuda & V. P. Glăveanu, eds., *The Palgrave Handbook of Social Creativity Research*. Cham: Palgrave Macmillan, pp. 569–584. https://doi.org/10.1007/978-3-319-95498-1_36

Dörfler, V., Stierand, M., & Chia, R. C. H. (2018, September 4–6). *Intellectual Quietness: Our Struggles with Researching Creativity as a Process*. BAM 2018: 32nd Annual Conference of the British Academy of Management, Bristol, UK. The British Academy of Management.

Dörfler, V. & Szendrey, J. (2008, April 28–30). *From Knowledge Management to Cognition Management: A Multi-Potential View of Cognition*. OLKC 2008: International Conference on Organizational Learning, Knowledge and Capabilities, Copenhagen. www.researchgate.net/publication/ 253780221

Dreyfus, H. L. & Dreyfus, S. E. (1986/2000). *Mind over Machine: The Power of Human Intuition and Expertise in the Era of the Computer*. New York: The Free Press.

Drucker, P. F. (1995). The Information Executives Truly Need. *Harvard Business Review*, **73**(1), 54–62. https://hbr.org/1995/01/the-information-executives-truly-need

Einstein, A. (2010). *The Ultimate Quotable Einstein*, edited by Alice Calaprice. Princeton, NJ: Princeton University Press. https://books.google.co.uk /books?id=G_iziBAPXtEC

Ericsson, K. A. & Charness, N. (1994). Expert Performance: Its Structure and Acquisition. *American Psychologist*, **49**(8), 725–747. https://doi.org/ 10.1037/0003-066X.49.8.725

Feigenbaum, E. A. (1977). *The Art of Artificial Intelligence: I. Themes and Case Studies of Knowledge Engineering*. 5th International Joint Conference on Artificial Intelligence,

Feigenbaum, E. A. (1992). *A Personal View of Expert Systems: Looking Back and Looking Ahead* (KSL 92–41). https://purl.stanford.edu/gr891tb5766

Feigenbaum, E. A. (2006). *Ed Feigenbaum's Search for AI*. Feigenfest 70th, Stanford University, Stanford, CA. https://youtu.be/B9zVdU3N7DY

Feigenbaum, E. A. & Simon, H. A. (1984). EPAM-Like Models of Recognition and Learning. *Cognitive Science*, **8**(4), 305–336. https://doi.org/10.1207/s15516709cog0804_1

Finley, K. (2012, October 1). Did Deep Blue Beat Kasparov because of a Computer Bug? *Wired*. www.wired.co.uk/article/deep-blue-bug

Fromm, E. (1942). *The Fear of Freedom*. London: Routledge.

Gardner, H. (1995). Why Would Anyone Become an Expert? "Expert Performance: Its Structure and Acquisition": Comment. *American Psychologist*, **50**(9), 802–803. https://doi.org/10.1037/0003-066X.50.9.802

Guo, E. & Hao, K. (2020, December 21). This Is the Stanford Vaccine Algorithm That Left Out Frontline Doctors. *MIT Technology Review*. www.technologyreview.com/2020/12/21/1015303

Handy, C. (2015). *The Second Curve: Thoughts on Reinventing Society*. London: Random House. https://books.google.hu/books?id=yztOBQAAQBAJ

Hao, K. (2019, February). Police across the US Are Training Crime-Predicting AIs on Falsified Data. *MIT Technology Review*. www.technologyreview.com/2019/02/13/137444

Heaven, D. (2019). Deep Trouble for Deep Learning. *Nature*, **574**(7777), 163–166. https://doi.org/10.1038/d41586-019-03013-5

Heaven, W. D. (2020, November 30). DeepMind's Protein-Folding AI Has Solved a 50-Year-Old Grand Challenge of Biology. *MIT Technology Review*. www.technologyreview.com/2020/11/30/1012712/

Hobbes, T. (1651/2018). *Leviathan*. London: Strelbytskyy Multimedia Publishing. https://books.google.co.uk/books?id=X81qDwAAQBAJ

Hofstadter, D. R. (1979/1999). *Godel, Escher, Bach: An Eternal Golden Braid*, 2nd ed. London: Basic Books.

Hume, D. (1739). *A Treatise of Human Nature*. London: John Noon. https://books.google.co.uk/books?id=66S3DAEACAAJ

Kahneman, D. (2011). *Thinking, Fast and Slow*. London: Penguin Books. http://books.google.co.uk/books?id=ZuKTvERuPG8C

Kelly, G. A. (1955/1963). *A Theory of Personality: The Psychology of Personal Constructs*, paperback ed. New York: Norton.

Keyes, D. (1966). *Flowers for Algernon*. Boston, MA: Harcourt, Brace & World. https://books.google.co.uk/books?id=_oG_iTxP1pIC

Knight, F. H. (1921). *Risk, Uncertainty and Profit*. New York: Houghton Mifflin. https://books.google.es/books?id=9fHTAAAAMAAJ

Kurzweil, R. (2005). *The Singularity Is Near: When Humans Transcend Biology*. Penguin Publishing Group. https://books.google.co.uk/books?id=9FtnppNpsT4C

Lave, J. & Wenger, E. C. (1991/2003). *Situated Learning: Legitimate Peripheral Participation.* New York: Cambridge University Press. http://books.google.co.uk/books?id=CAVIOrW3vYAC

LeCun, Y., Bengio, Y., & Hinton, G. (2015). Deep Learning. *Nature,* **521**(7553), 436–444. https://doi.org/10.1038/nature14539

Lenat, D. B. & Feigenbaum, E. A. (1991). On the Thresholds of Knowledge. *Artificial Intelligence,* **47**(1), 185–250. https://doi.org/10.1016/0004-3702(91)90055-O

Liu, C. (2020). *The World's First Trillionaires and More AI Predictions.* AoM Insights. https://journals.aom.org/doi/abs/10.5465/ambpp.2019.12809 symposium.summary

March, J. G. (1994). *Primer on Decision Making: How Decisions Happen.* New York: Free Press. http://books.google.nl/books?id=zydIx15DM2kC

McCorduck, P. (2004). *Machines Who Think: A Personal Inquiry into the History and Prospects of Artificial Intelligence,* 2nd ed. Natick, MA: A. K. Peters. https://monoskop.org/images/1/1e/McCorduck_Pamela_Machines_Who_Think_2nd_ed.pdf

McCulloch, W. S. & Pitts, W. (1943). A Logical Calculus of the Ideas Immanent in Nervous Activity. *Bulletin of Mathematical Biophysics,* **5**(4), 115–133. https://doi.org/10.1007/BF02478259

McGilchrist, I. (2019). *The Master and His Emissary: The Divided Brain and the Making of the Western World,* 2nd ed. New Haven, CT: Yale University Press. https://books.google.co.uk/books?id=alSIDwAAQBAJ

Mérő, L. (1990). *Ways of Thinking: The Limits of Rational Thought and Artificial Intelligence.* New Jersey, NJ: World Scientific.

Meyer, J., Land, R., & Baillie, C. (2010). *Threshold Concepts and Transformational Learning.* Rotterdam: Sense Publishers. https://books.google.co.uk/books?id=AOqaSQAACAAJ

Minsky, M. L. (1988). *The Society of Mind.* New York: Simon & Schuster.

Minsky, M. L. (2006). *The Emotion Machine: Commonsense Thinking, Artificial Intelligence, and the Future of the Human Mind.* New York: Simon & Schuster.

Moggridge, B. (2007). The Internet: Interviews with Terry Winograd, Larry Page and Sergey Brin of Google, Steve Rogers, and Mark Podlaseck. In B. Moggridge, ed., *Designing Interactions.* Cambridge, MA: MIT Press.

Musk, E. (2018, April 17). *Elon Musk on Google DeepMind.* YouTube. https://youtu.spenbe/MuWWZ91-G6w

von Neumann, J. & Morgenstern, O. (1953). *Theory of Games and Economic Behavior,* 3rd ed. New York: John Wiley & Sons.

Newell, A., Shaw, J. C., & Simon, H. A. (1963). Empirical Explorations with the Logic Theory Machine: A Case Study in Heuristics. In E. A. Feigenbaum & J. Feldman, eds., *Computers and Thought*. New York: McGraw-Hill, Inc., pp. 109–133.

Newell, A. & Simon, H. A. (1956). The Logic Theory Machine: A Complex Information Processing System. *IRE Transactions on Information Theory*, **2** (3), 61–79. https://doi.org/10.1109/TIT.1956.1056797

Oliver, N., Calvard, T., & Potočnik, K. (2017a). Cognition, Technology, and Organizational Limits: Lessons from the Air France 447 Disaster. *Organization Science*, **28**(4), 729–743. https://doi.org/10.1287/orsc.2017 .1138

Oliver, N., Calvard, T., & Potočnik, K. (2017b, September 15). The Tragic Crash of Flight AF447 Shows the Unlikely but Catastrophic Consequences of Automation. *Harvard Business Review*. https://hbr.org/2017/09/the-tragic-crash-of-flight-af447-shows-the-unlikely-but-catastrophic-consequences-of-automation

Pavlov, I. P. (1927). *Conditioned Reflexes: An Investigation of the Physiological Activity of the Cerebral Cortex*. London: Routledge and Kegan Paul. http://psychclassics.yorku.ca/Pavlov

Polányi, M. (1946). *Science, Faith and Society*. London: Oxford University Press.

Polányi, M. (1959). *The Study of Man*. Chicago, IL: University of Chicago Press. http://books.google.rs/books?id=lbMkAQAAMAAJ

Polányi, M. (1962a/2002). *Personal Knowledge: Towards a Post-Critical Philosophy*. London: Routledge.

Polányi, M. (1962b). Tacit Knowing: Its Bearing on Some Problems of Philosophy. *Reviews of Modern Physics*, **34**(4), 601–616. http://link.aps.org /doi/10.1103/RevModPhys.34.601

Polányi, M. (1966a). The Logic of Tacit Inference. *Philosophy*, **41**(155), 1–18. https://doi.org/10.1017/S0031819100066110

Polányi, M. (1966b/1983). *The Tacit Dimension*. Gloucester, MA: Peter Smith. https://books.google.co.uk/books?id=zfsb-eZHPy0C

Polányi, M. (1969). *Knowing and Being*. Chicago, IL: University of Chicago Press.

Popper, K. R. (1968/2004). *The Logic of Scientific Discovery*, 2nd ed. London: Routledge. https://archive.org/details/PopperLogicScientificDiscovery/page/n3

Pyrko, I., Dörfler, V., & Eden, C. (2017). Thinking Together: What Makes Communities of Practice Work? *Human Relations*, **70**(4), 389–409. https://doi.org/10.1177/0018726716661040

Ransbotham, S., Kiron, D., Gerbert, P., & Reeves, M. (2017, September). *Reshaping Business with Artificial Intelligence: Closing the Gap between Ambition and Action*. MIT Sloan Management Review and The Boston Consulting Group.

Roszak, T. (1986/1994). *The Cult of Information: A Neo-Luddite Treatise on High-Tech, Artificial Intelligence, and the True Art of Thinking*. London: University of California Press.

Rumelhart, D. E. & Norman, D. A. (1988). Representation in Memory. In R. C. Atkinson, R. J. Herrnstein, G. Lindzey, & R. D. Luce, eds., *Stevens' Handbook of Experimental Psychology*, 2nd ed., Vol. 2, *Learning and Cognition*. New York: John Wiley & Sons, pp. 511–587.

Russell, S. & Norvig, P. (2020). *Artificial Intelligence: A Modern Approach*, 4th ed. Harlow: Pearson Education. http://aima.cs.berkeley.edu

Searle, J. R. (1980). Minds, Brains, and Programs. *Behavioral and Brain Sciences*, **3**(3), 417–424. https://doi.org/10.1017/S0140525X00005756

Searle, J. R. (1998). *The Mystery of Consciousness*. London: Granta Books.

Selfridge, O. G. (1955). *Pattern Recognition in Modern Computers*. Western Joint Computer Conference, Los Angeles, CA.

Shubik, M. (1954). Information, Risk, Ignorance and Indeterminacy. *Quarterly Journal of Economics*, **68**(4), 629–640. https://doi.org/10.2307/1881881

Simon, H. A. (1977). *The New Science of Management Decision*, 3rd ed. New Jersey, NJ: Prentice-Hall.

Simon, H. A. (1991). *Models of My Life*. New York: Basic Books. https://books.google.co.uk/books?id=dFgwBQAAQBAJ

Simon, H. A. (1995). Artificial Intelligence: An Empirical Science. *Artificial Intelligence*, **77**(1), 95–127. https://doi.org/10.1016/0004-3702(95)

Simon, H. A. (1996). *The Sciences of the Artificial*, 3rd ed. Cambridge, MA: MIT Press.

Simon, H. A. & Feigenbaum, E. A. (1964). An Information-Processing Theory of Some Effects of Similarity, Familiarization, and Meaningfulness in Verbal Learning. *Journal of Verbal Learning and Verbal Behavior*, **3**(5), 385–396. https://doi.org/10.1016/S0022-5371(64)80007-4

Simon, H. A. & Newell, A. (1958). Heuristic Problem Solving: The Next Advance in Operations Research. *Operations Research*, **6**(1), 1–10. https://doi.org/10.1287/opre.6.1.1

Sinclair, M. & Ashkanasy, N. M. (2005). Intuition: Myth or a Decision-Making Tool? *Management Learning*, **36**(3), 353–370. https://doi.org/10.1177/1350507605055351

Skinner, B. F. (1950). Are Theories of Learning Necessary? *Psychological Review*, **57**(4), 193–216. https://doi.org/10.1037/h0054367

Sowden, P. T., Pringle, A., & Peacock, M. (2020). Verbal Protocol Analysis as a Tool to Understand the Creative Process. In V. Dörfler & M. Stierand, eds., *Handbook of Research Methods on Creativity*. Cheltenham: Edward Elgar, pp. 314–328. https://doi.org/10.4337/9781786439659.00033

Spender, J. C. (2014). *Business Strategy: Managing Uncertainty, Opportunity, and Enterprise*. Oxford, UK: Oxford University Press. https://books.google.co.uk/books?id=RNxMAgAAQBAJ

Spender, J. C. (2015, August 4). Stop Worrying about Whether Machines Are "Intelligent." *Harvard Business Review*. https://hbr.org/2015/08/stop-worrying-about-whether-machines-are-intelligent

Spender, J. C. (2018). Managing: According to Williamson, or to Coase? *Kindai Management Review*, **6**, 13–34. www.kindai.ac.jp/files/rd/research-center/management-innovation/kindai-management-review/vol6_2.pdf

Spender, J. C. (2021). Towards a Firm for Our Time. *Kindai Management Review*, **9**, 124–137.

Stierand, M. (2015). Developing Creativity in Practice: Explorations with World-Renowned Chefs. *Management Learning*, **46**(5), 598–617. https://doi.org/10.1177/1350507614560302

Stierand, M. & Dörfler, V. (2016). The Role of Intuition in the Creative Process of Expert Chefs. *Journal of Creative Behavior*, **50**(3), 178–185. https://doi.org/10.1002/jocb.100

Tesla, N. (1919/2006). *My Inventions: The Autobiography of Nikola Tesla*. Milton Keynes: Filiquarian Publishing.

Turing, A. M. (1937). On Computable Numbers, with an Application to the Entscheidungsproblem. *Proceedings of the London Mathematical Society*, **s2–42**(1), 230–265. https://doi.org/10.1112/plms/s2-42.1.230

Turing, A. M. (1950). Computing Machinery and Intelligence. *Mind*, **59**(236), 433–460. https://doi.org/10.1093/mind/LIX.236.433

Ullman, S. (2019). Using Neuroscience to Develop Artificial Intelligence. *Science*, **363**(6428), 692–693. https://doi.org/10.1126/science.aau6595

Velencei, J. (2017, March 9–10). *Modelling the Reality of Decision Making with the Doctus Knowledge-Based System*. 20th International Scientific Conference, "Enterprise and Competitive Environment," Brno, Czech Republic.

Warwick, K. & Shah, H. (2016). Can Machines Think? A Report on Turing Test Experiments at the Royal Society. *Journal of Experimental & Theoretical Artificial Intelligence*, **28**(6), 989–1007. https://doi.org/10.1080/0952813X.2015.1055826

Weizenbaum, J. (1966). ELIZA – A Computer Program for the Study of Natural Language Communication Between Man and Machine. *Communications of the ACM*, **9**(1), 36–45. https://doi.org/10.1145/365153.365168

Weizenbaum, J. (1976). *Computer Power and Human Reason: From Judgment to Calculation*. New York: W. H. Freeman & Co. https://books.google.co.uk /books?id=3yfyAAAACAAJ

Whitehead, A. N. & Russell, B. A. (1927). *Principia Mathematica*, 2nd ed., Vol. 1. Cambridge, UK: Cambridge University Press. https://books.google.co.uk /books?id=ke9yGmFy24sC

Wiklund, J. (2020). Working in Bed – A Commentary on "Automation, Algorithms, and Beyond: Why Work Design Matters More than Ever in a Digital World" by Parker and Grote. *Applied Psychology*. https://doi.org/ 10.1111/apps.12261

Wilczek, F. (2015). *A Beautiful Question: Finding Nature's Deep Design*: Penguin Books Limited. https://books.google.co.uk/books?id=Oh3ICAA AQBAJ

Winograd, T. (1980). What Does It Mean to Understand Language? *Cognitive Science*, **4**(3), 209–241. https://doi.org/10.1207/s15516709cog0403_1

Winograd, T. (1990). Thinking Machines: Can There Be? Are We? In D. Partridge & Y. Wilks, eds., *The Foundations of Artificial Intelligence: A Sourcebook*. Cambridge, UK: Cambridge University Press, pp. 167–189. https://doi.org/10.1017/CBO9780511663116.017

Wittgenstein, L. J. J. (1969). *On Certainty*, trans. D. Paul & G. E. M. Anscombe. Oxford: Blackwell.

Zadeh, L. A. (1965). Fuzzy Sets. *Information and Control*, **8**(3), 338–353. https://doi.org/10.1016/S0019-9958(65)90241-X

Cambridge Elements $\overline{\overline{}}$

Business Strategy

Elements in the series

A full series listing is available at: www.cambridge.org/EBUS